THE
ENCYCLOPEDIA
OF
SEWING
TECHNIQUES

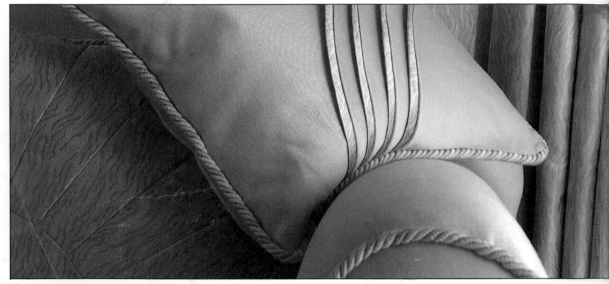

Photograph by Interior Selection Ltd.

T H E

E N C Y C L O P E D I A

OF

SEWING

T E C H N I Q U E S

JAN EATON

BARRON'S

Woodbury, New York • Toronto

A QUARTO BOOK

First U.S. edition published in 1987 by
Barron's Educational Series, Inc.
Barron's Educational Series, Inc. has exclusive publication
rights in the English language in the U.S.A., its territories, and
possessions, and Canada.

Copyright © 1986 Quarto Publishing

International Standard Book No. 0-8120-5815-1

Library of Congress Catalog Card No. 86-26514

This book was designed and produced by
Quarto Publishing Ltd
The Old Brewery,
6 Blundell Street
London N7 9BH

Senior Editor: Helen Owen
Editor: Jane Laing
Art Editor: Hazel Edington
Designer: Richard Mellor/Worthington Design Co.
Design Assistant: Ursula Dawson
Illustrator: Mary Horner
Photographer: John Heseltine
Indexer: Richard Bird
Art Director: Peter Laws
Editorial Director: Jim Miles

Typeset by Burbeck Associates Limited, Harlow, Essex
Manufactured in Hong Kong by
Regent Publishing Services Limited
Printed by Leefung-Asco Printers Limited, Hong Kong

C O N T E N T S

CONTENTS

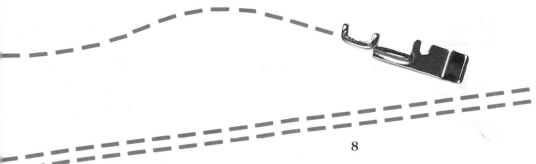

There is a wide range of sewing machines

designed especially for home use.

At first sight, choosing a sewing machine

seems to be a totally bewildering task!

This chapter describes the different types of

machines available and deals in detail with

the machine controls and essential sewing

equipment. It shows you how to begin using

your new machine, and how to give your

sewing a professional finish.

A simple zigzag machine with a free arm, semi-automatic buttonhole and a choice of stretch stitches will be adequate for most dressmaking and home sewing needs. A heavier type of machine with good needle penetration and a slow stitch control would be better for heavy fabrics and tailoring processes. If you have to pack your machine away after each sewing session, choose a portable, lightweight model that is easy to lift. Other machines have a range of decorative features, but they will be much more expensive. It is worthwhile remembering that no single machine will include all the features offered by the different manufacturers, so you must decide which features are essential to you.

SEWING MACHINES

The first step when choosing a sewing machine is to decide which type of machine will suit your particular needs, as they fall into quite distinct categories.

The next thing to consider is price. A good sewing machine may seem rather expensive, but a well-made machine will last a lifetime if properly cared for and serviced regularly. Decide how much you want to spend and then look for the most suitable machine in that price range. You should buy your machine from a reputable dealer who offers a thorough demonstration and good after-sale service. Many dealers can provide additional instruction for a complicated machine if necessary. If you do decide to buy a machine from a discount store or by mail order, you may have trouble getting it serviced elsewhere.

Try out as many machines as you can that look suitable, using scraps of your own fabric. Take along a selection of different weights and types of fabric, including a thin, slippery synthetic and a stretchy knit, for these can be difficult to sew on some machines. Stitch through double fabric and check that the machine stitches evenly without allowing the fabric to 'creep' under the foot. Ask the demonstrator to show you the stretch stitches and those for finishing raw edges. Try out the threading and bobbin-winding procedures for ease of use. Other features to look at include the position of the light, which should be directly over the needle, the quality of the instruction book, and also the response of the control.

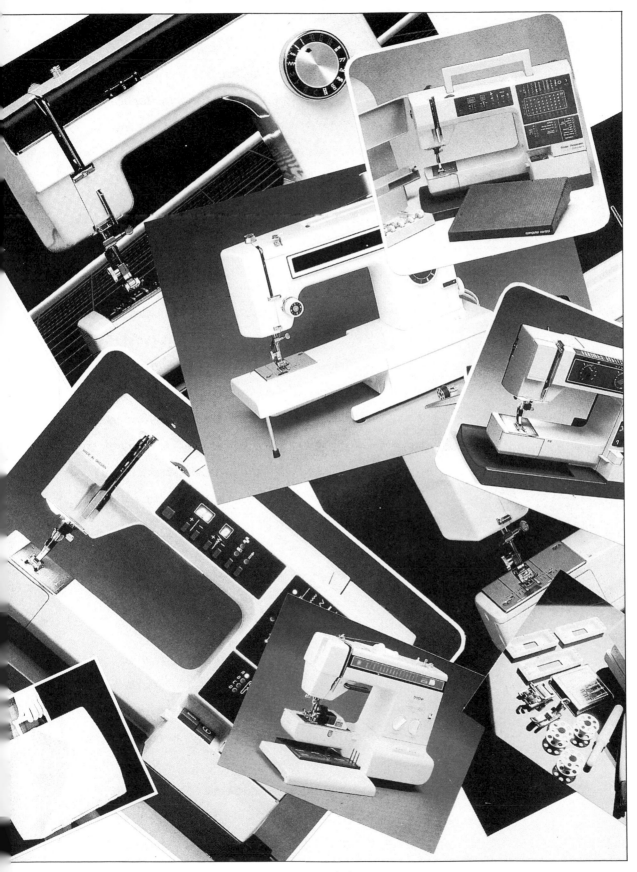

STRAIGHT STITCH

These are the simplest type of machines available and are now made by very few manufacturers. These machines sew varying lengths of straight stitch forward or in reverse and, although very limited in scope, are generally reliable. They have a flat bed around the stitching area to provide support for the fabric.

BASIC ZIGZAG

In addition to the usual straight stitch these machines will work an adjustable zigzag stitch, up to ¼inch (5mm) wide. The length of the stitch is also adjustable – a very short length produces a satin stitch, which can be used for working buttonholes, with the fabric guided manually. Straight stitching can usually be done with the needle to the right, center or left of the needle hole in the foot. These machines have either a flat bed or a free arm, which is useful when stitching openings and small circular areas such as sleeves and cuffs. There are controls for stitch length and width, a pushbutton reverse, and a limited range of feet and attachments.

SEMI-AUTOMATIC

Semi-automatic machines have more useful features than the basic zigzag type, and they can also do simple decorative stitches. They have straight and zigzag stitch facilities, variable needle positions, pushbutton reverse, and the usual stitch length and width controls. In addition, they have pattern cams which alter the width control automatically to form simple, decorative stitches based on a satin stitch. The pattern cams are either inserted manually inside the machine or selected by a knob or lever on the outside. The patterns are based on geometric and curved shapes and they can be worked on a close satin stitch setting or opened up by use of the stitch length lever. These machines also offer a semi-automatic buttonhole. The stitch still has to be reversed manually at the end, but the width of the satin stitch is preset by turning a dial. They also have a wider range of feet and attachments and are available as either flat-bed or free-arm models.

AUTOMATIC

The definition of an automatic sewing machine is one which has a built-in buttonholer, which automatically reverses at the chosen point. The button-hole is worked in two, four or five steps and the width of the satin stitch is preset. This definition means that a machine with an automatic buttonholer and a few utility stitches comes into the same category as a machine with many more advanced features such as automatic patterns and special straight stitch for stretch fabric. With the advanced machines, the fabric is moved backward and forward beneath the needle, and the needle bar may move from side to side as well, depending on the automatic stitch selected. This gives a range of stretch and overlock utility stitches and a large choice of decorative stitches. New models of this type wind the bobbin through the needle to save unthreading the machine.

SERGERS

Sergers, also called overlock sewing machines, allow home sewers to reproduce ready-to-wear with ease. These machines stitch, trim, and overcast a seam in one step at twice the speed of a conventional sewing machine. Every major sewing machine manufacturer now has a model of its own and they are proving immensely popular.

ELECTRONIC

Electronic machines have all the features of the advanced automatic machines, including mechanical pattern cams, but by the use of electronics they make the physical process of stitching easier. They have an integrated circuit, located either in the machine or in the foot control, which controls the mechanical functions. Some machines use both a circuit in the machine and one in the foot control. An electronic foot control regulates the speed of the motor and provides full needle power even at slow speeds or when stitching heavyweight fabric. It allows more sensitive control and has the ability to stop and start immediately. The circuit in the machine provides for stitch-by-stitch sewing, allowing the machine to stop with the needle either up or down.

COMPUTERIZED

These are the most sophisticated machines available; they are controlled by a built-in micro-processor. They have a full range of features including a one-step buttonhole, but their real advantage is their wide range of decorative options. There are no mechanically operated pattern cams, as the stitch patterns are stored in the computer memory. The stitch patterns are chosen by touching a button, and the selection is then shown on a visual display panel. Pre-programmed motifs and alphabets can be elongated or shortened without losing the density of the stitches, and they can be inverted or stitched in mirror image. A sequence of stitch patterns can be chosen and dialed into the machine, which will then repeat the sequence exactly.

MACHINE CONTROLS

Machine controls may look different from machine to machine but their basic functions are the same. All sewing machines require a continuous thread to be fed to the needle at the correct tension and connected to another tensioned thread from the bobbin. These two threads form the lock stitch, which is the basis of all machine stitches. The spool pin, located on the top of the machine, holds the spool of thread for the needle and allows it to unwind evenly. Some machines have more than one spool pin to allow twin and triple needles to be used.

Thread Guide

Tension Disc

Machine Foot

Needleplate

BOBBIN WINDER

The bobbin winding position differs according to the machine, but the thread always passes through a tension control to insure even winding. The hand wheel is disengaged in order to wind the bobbin. Many machines automatically stop winding when the bobbin is full, and on some sophisticated machines the bobbin can be wound directly through the needle without unthreading.

HAND WHEEL

The machine is worked by turning the hand wheel which is usually driven by an electric motor. The hand wheel can be turned by hand to make a single stitch or to raise or lower the needle.

FOOT CONTROLS

Foot controls can be electric, electronic, or worked by air pressure control.

FEET

All machines, except the straight stitch type, have at least two feet provided with them, one for straight stitch and one for zigzag. Some machines have a selection of special purpose feet that come as standard, while others have a range that can be purchased separately. The feet are hinged to accommodate different weights of fabric, and they can be screwed in place or clipped onto a shank.

Bobbin Winder

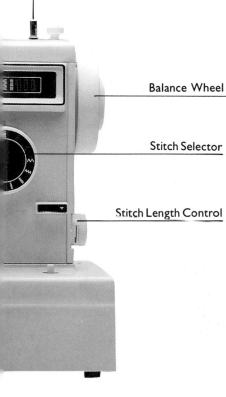

Balance Wheel

Stitch Selector

Stitch Length Control

NEEDLE

The needle is fixed into the needle bar by a small screw which should be tightened firmly after inserting the needle.

PRESSER BAR LIFTER

This is a lever positioned behind and above the foot that raises and lowers the foot. The thread tension is engaged only when the foot is lowered.

PRESSER BAR

The presser bar holds the presser foot and often incorporates a thread cutter at the back of the bar. The pressure can be adjusted to suit different fabric weights.

BOBBINS AND BOBBIN CASES

Bobbins are circular and vary in size according to the machine, so they are not usually interchangeable. The bobbin thread feeds through an adjustable tension spring on the bobbin case. The bobbin fits snugly into the bobbin case, which either slots in under the needle plate or is inserted from the front or side. On some machines there is no separate case; the bobbin is dropped into a fixed case.

STITCH SELECTOR

If the machine features a few utility and pattern stitches, the controls are usually incorporated into the stitch width dial, which will be marked with the appropriate symbols. Automatic machines have a pattern panel with a lever or movable pointer that selects the stitches.

TAKE-UP LEVER AND THREAD GUIDES

The thread feeds through the eye in the take-up lever and down to the needle. Thread guides are small loops of wire that guide the thread from the spool to the needle. Some machines have a slotted take-up lever and thread guides to make threading quick and simple.

STITCH LENGTH CONTROL

The length of stitch is determined by the rate at which the fabric is fed under the foot by the feed dog, which is regulated by the stitch length control. This control can be a graduated lever or a numbered dial. The feed dog can be dropped or covered on most machines for darning and free embroidery.

STITCH WIDTH CONTROL

This control is found on all machines except the straight stitch type. It controls the width of the zigzag and decorative stitches and may be a graduated lever or a numbered dial. Some machines have a dial or lever marked left, middle, and right, which allows the needle to be set in one of these positions.

TENSION CONTROL

The tension control is located on the front of the machine or partially concealed on the top. It contains disks, which act like brakes and control the rate at which the thread feeds to the needle. The tension is altered by a numbered dial or by a plus and minus indicator. There may be an extra control for sewing with two threads.

NEEDLE PLATE

The needle plate surrounds the feed dog and has a small hole for straight stitch and a slot for zigzag stitch. There may be two separate plates provided with the machine; these are changed according to the type of stitching in progress, or there may be one plate which can be turned around. The plate is held in position magnetically or by screws or clips, and has fabric guide markings.

CONTROLS ON COMPUTERIZED MACHINES

All the functions are chosen by touch control, either alone or in conjunction with dialing wheels for stitch length and width. Stop, start, reverse, stitch selection and buttonhole symbols are shown on a central selector panel.

MACHINE NEEDLES AND THREAD

NEEDLES

Modern machine needles have a rounded shank which is flattened down one side and has a long groove on the opposite side. Thread the needle from the grooved side. Do not use a blunt or bent needle. Needles are made in various sizes to accommodate all weights of thread, and there are different types for specific purposes. Use the correct size needle for the fabric and change the needle frequently, especially when working with synthetics.

Basic sharp point needles are used for most general sewing purposes on woven fabrics.

Ballpoint needles are specially designed for sewing synthetic knitted fabric. The rounded point passes between the threads of the fabric without splitting the yarn.

Jean needles are elongated and have a very sharp point. They are strong enough to penetrate the hard texture of denim and canvas.

Wedge-point needles have a sharpened, wedge-shaped tip to cut cleanly through leather, suede, and vinyl. Never use this type of needle on fabric.

Twin and triple needles are multiple needles for pin tucks and double or triple line stitching.

Wing needles have a wide blade which makes a hole in the fabric; they are used only for decorative stitching. A double wing needle has one wing needle and one ordinary needle fixed together.

Perfect stitch needles have a long indentation near the eye. They are used on fine synthetic fabrics to help prevent skipped stitches.

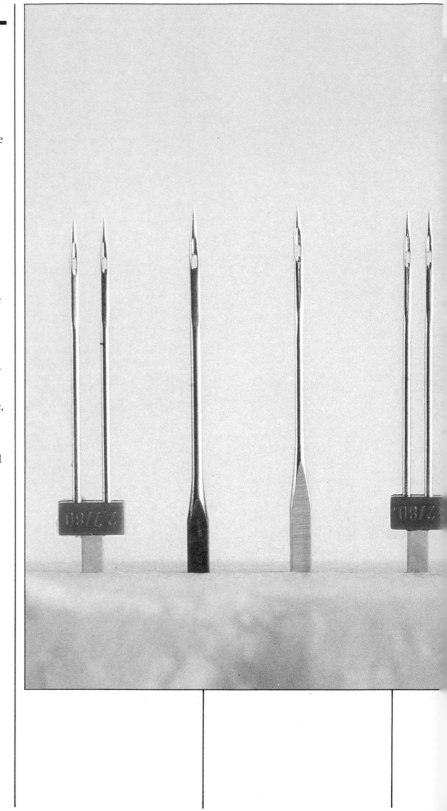

THREAD

Select a thread according to the type of fabric you are using. Cotton-wrapped polyester is suitable for most fabrics; it has the strength and "give" of pure polyester but can take the hot iron required for cotton and linen material. Pure polyester and mercerized cotton can be used for synthetics and natural-fiber

NEEDLE AND THREAD SELECTION CHART		
Fabric	**Thread**	**Needle**
Lightweight Chiffon, organza, fine lace, lawn, voile	Silk, mercerized cotton, extra fine (any fiber), size 60-100	70
Medium weight Velvet, gingham, crepe, brocade, linen, fine denims, polyester/cotton	Polyester, cotton-wrapped polyester, mercerized cotton, size 50-60	80
Heavy Wide rib corduroy, tweed, heavy woolens	Polyester, cotton-wrapped polyester, heavy duty (any fiber), size 30-40	90 or 100
Very heavy Canvas, upholstery fabric, heavy denim	Polyester, cotton-wrapped polyester, heavy duty (any fiber), size 20	100 or 110

fabrics, respectively. Silk thread is ideal for silk fabrics. Match the color of the thread to that of the fabric, choosing one shade darker, because the thread will appear lighter when stitched.

On all types of thread, the higher the number on the spool, the finer the thread. Select the number of the thread according to the weight of the fabric.

MACHINE ATTACHMENTS

All machines have special attachments for different types of stitching. Some make sewing difficult fabrics easier, some save time and some are used in conjunction with a particular needle. Your machine handbook will give details of those available for your machine and show you how to attach them. Some will come with your machine, while others will have to be bought separately. Attachments are usually a good investment, because they will lend a more professional appearance to the items you make. A selection of machine attachments is shown below.

ZIPPER FOOT

A zipper foot is supplied with most modern machines. It is also used to attach cording and is designed for stitching close to the zipper teeth or the filled edge of cording. On some machines the needle position adjusts so that it will fit into the indentations on each side of the foot; on other models the zipper foot is adjusted to fit to the needle. Special grooved plastic zipper feet are also available for use with an invisible zipper.

EMBROIDERY FOOT

An embroidery foot is made from clear plastic so that you can see what is happening underneath it. A groove is cut out underneath the foot to allow the thickness of the stitching to pass through it without becoming flattened. Use this foot for all satin stitch and decorative stitching.

BINDING FOOT

This foot applies pre-folded bias binding to raw edges. Use purchased binding or make your own from bias strips of fabric using a tape maker.

HEMMER FOOT

A hemmer foot rolls under the raw edge of the fabric to form a narrow double hem which is fed under the needle. This attachment works best with lightweight fabrics.

PIN TUCK FOOT

This foot accommodates narrow tucks in the fabric which fit into the grooves under the foot; it is used with a twin needle.

GATHERING FOOT

A gathering foot will gather a length of fabric in fixed amounts as you stitch. It can be used to gather a single piece of fabric, or to gather a ruffle and attach it to another piece of fabric in one operation.

ROLLER FOOT

A roller foot has two or more grooved rollers fitted into the front and back of the foot. Use it when stitching leather, plastic, velvet and slippery fabrics.

OVERLOCK FOOT

This foot is used with stitches that make a seam and finish the raw edges of the fabric in one operation. It is a useful extra to buy if you make a lot of garments and you like this type of seam finish.

STARTING TO SEW

When you have bought your new sewing machine, learn to control it by practicing stitching on paper and then on scraps of fabric. Do not thread the machine at this stage. Put a sheet of lined or graph paper under the foot, lower the foot and start to stitch along the lines. Practice stitching lines, curves, and corners, reversing, changing speed, and stopping and starting at marked points on the paper.

When you feel confident about your control, thread the machine according to the diagram in the handbook and practice the same techniques on a double piece of fabric. Use your hands to guide the fabric gently under the foot without pushing or pulling it. Try out all the various utility stitches and adjust the stitch length and width to see what will happen.

NEEDLE THREAD TOO LOOSE	NEEDLE THREAD CORRECT TENSION	NEEDLE THREAD TOO TIGHT
When the needle thread is too loose, it will be pulled in loops to the underside of the fabric by the bobbin thread. The stitching will be loose and will break easily. Correct this by lowering the foot and then turning the tension dial to a higher number or toward the plus sign.	When the two threads are tensioned correctly, the link formed between the threads is centered between the fabric layers. Equal amounts of needle and bobbin thread have been used, and the stitching lies flat without puckering or distorting the fabric. A seam stitched with a balanced tension is much stronger than one stitched with an unbalanced tension.	When the tension of the needle thread is tighter than that of the bobbin thread, puckers will occur in the fabric along the stitched line. The bobbin thread is drawn tightly to the top of the fabric and may even be visible on this side. To correct this, lower the foot and then turn the tension dial to a lower number or toward the minus sign.

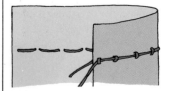

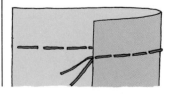

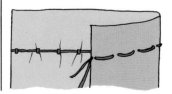

KEEPING STRAIGHT

At this point, you are ready to begin your first sewn item. Pick something simple to make and at first use just straight and zigzag stitches. Always have a guideline along which to sew: a line of basting, a chalk line, or an edge. Do not stitch directly on top of basting, but slightly to one side, toward the raw edge, so that the basting can be removed easily after the stitching is finished. Keep stitching straight by running the edge of the fabric even with the presser foot or by using the guide marked on the needle plate. Work from the wider end of the piece of fabric and stitch the seams in the same direction if possible.

SECURING THREAD ENDS

It is important to finish the thread ends securely at each end of the stitching. Do this by reversing the direction of the stitching. Start stitching about ⅜ inch (1cm) from the edge and reverse to the edge before stitching forward. At the end of the line, when you are approaching the point where you want to stop, put your hand on the hand wheel to act as a brake and ease off the pressure on the foot control. All machines will stop within one or two stitches. You can use the wheel to make the final stitch by hand. Do not stitch beyond the edge of the fabric. Reverse the stitching for ⅜ inch (1cm) to secure the threads. Then, cut off the surplus at each end of the stitching. When using a fine fabric, fasten off the threads by hand, by running the threads through the stitching on the wrong side with a needle. On fine fabrics reverse stitching tends to pucker and should be avoided.

TURNING CORNERS

When you reach the corner point, turn the hand wheel, if necessary, so that the needle is lowered into the fabric. Raise the foot and pivot the fabric around the needle so that you can stitch along the seamline. Lower the foot and continue stitching.

On fine fabrics and those which are likely to fray, adjust the stitch to a smaller size just before turning the corner. Work a few stitches past the corner, then return to the original stitch size.

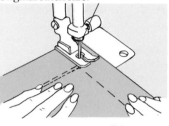

STITCHING AROUND CURVES

On a gentle curve, stitch as usual, but use a slow speed and ease the fabric around gradually. For a tight curve, stop stitching at the beginning of the curve and lower the needle into the fabric. Raise the foot and turn the fabric slightly in the direction of the curve. Work one or two stitches slowly and then repeat the "stop, turn, stitch" sequence right around the curve. Take care to keep the stitching at an even distance from the edge of the fabric.

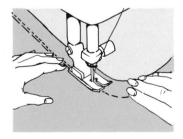

When you feel really familiar with your machine, try out the more complicated features such as buttonholes and any automatic stitch patterns. Practice them on a scrap of fabric a few times before using them on a project.

GENERAL RULES FOR MACHINE STITCHING

Follow the suggestions given below to obtain a good finish with machine stitching:
● Before stitching press the fabric, using the correct iron temperature, so that it is perfectly flat and smooth.
● Use the correct size and type of needle for the fabric and the stitch.
● Change needles frequently, as they soon become blunt.
● Use the same color and type of thread for the needle and bobbin.
● Set the stitch length and width to settings that seem suitable. Try out the stitching on a folded piece of extra fabric. Press and check both sides of the fabric to see if any adjustments are necessary. If so, make the adjustments and test the stitching again.
● When using knitted, stretchy fabric, pull it gently to make sure the zigzag width is sufficient to prevent the stitches from snapping.
● After stitching, press the line of stitches on one side of the fabric to flatten and set them into the fabric.
● Trim off any loose, fraying threads from the edges of the fabric.

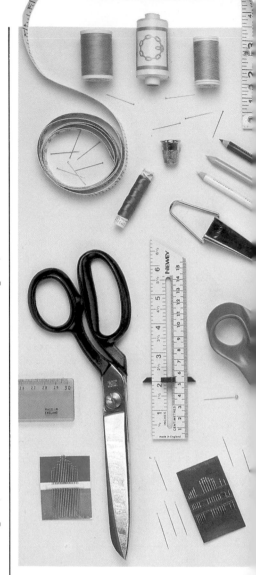

Good equipment helps to give a more professional finish to your sewing. A few basic pieces of equipment are essential, so always buy the best you can afford. There is an increasing range of gadgets available which, strictly speaking, are not essential, although many of them are useful and timesaving.

SCISSORS

Good quality scissors are a real investment, for they will cut accurately and last longer than cheaper ones. Buy several pairs in different sizes and make sure they are comfortable to hold. Drop-forged scissors are quite heavy, but they can be sharpened repeatedly and, with care, they will last a lifetime. Lightweight stainless steel scissors with plastic handles are comfortable to use and keep sharp for a long time.

Choose a large pair of scissors with 11 inch (28cm) blades for cutting out fabric. These should be shaped so that the blade rests flat on the table while you are cutting. A medium-sized pair, 4 to 5 inches (10 to 12cm) long, are useful for trimming seams and cutting small pieces of fabric. A small pair will also be needed for trimming thread ends, clipping fabric edges and cutting buttonholes. Pinking shears for finishing the edges of fabric are useful, but not essential. Look after your scissors and do not cut anything other than fabric with them, or they will become blunt.

BODKINS

A bodkin is used for inserting elastic or cord through a casing. (It is also handy for removing basting stitches and easing out corners and points to give a sharp finish.) The elastic is tied securely round the groove at the end of the bodkin, and then inserted. An elastic threader, which is a flat, blunt-ended metal needle with a very large eye, is also used for threading elastic through a casting.

THIMBLES

A thimble is worn on the middle finger of the hand that holds the needle. It enables you to push the needle through the fabric painlessly, which is important if the fabric is stiff or has a very close weave.

NEEDLES

The choice of needles for hand sewing is largely a matter of personal preference. Needles are designed for specific purposes, but you may feel comfortable using a certain type.

Betweens are short needles used for most types of hand sewing, especially hemming.

Sharps are longer and are used for basting and gathering, when more than one stitch is on the needle.

Milliner's needles are very long and are used for stitching through many layers of fabric.

Keep a range of types and sizes of needles and replace them frequently, as they soon become blunt from use. Select the needle size according to the weight of fabric and thread you are using.

PINS

Buy good quality pins in a container. Long pins with glass or plastic heads are useful when working with openweave or hairy fabrics, as they are easy to see. Ballpoint pins should be used when working with silk. It is useful to keep a pincushion or magnetic pinholder by the machine.

Buy a fiberglass tape measure marked with standard and metric measurements. Fabric and plastic tape measures may eventually stretch. A wooden yardstick is essential for accurate long measurements and for marking hems. A metal or plastic seam gauge should also be purchased. This has a movable pointer and can be used when making tucks and pleats and for marking buttonholes. A plastic right-angled triangle and a ruler are needed for altering paper patterns.

TAILOR'S CHALK

Tailor's chalk is used to mark stitching lines, darts, and hem-lines. Use white chalk, since this is the easiest to brush out after stitching. Keep the edge of the chalk sharp by paring it carefully with a blade. Chalk pencils have a brush at one end for removing the chalk marks from the fabric. A fabric-marking pen with special ink which washes out can also be used to mark single layers of fabric, although it has been found that this may rot some fabrics.

OTHER SEWING EQUIPMENT

The following items are not essential, but they will all save time and make certain processes easier. A skirt marker will help you mark a hemline by puffing a chalk line onto the garment at a chosen height from the floor. A loop turner is useful for turning narrow bias tubing. Battery-operated scissors are quicker but less accurate than ordinary ones. A needle threader is handy if your eyesight is less than perfect. Dressmaker's carbon paper and a tracing wheel can be used to transfer symbols from a paper pattern to fabric. Iron-on fusible web will hold hems and facings in place. Perforated fusible waistbandings will make the construction of cuffs and waistbands simpler.

THREAD

Several types of thread are available for both machine and hand sewing.
Mercerized cotton thread is smooth and has a slight sheen; it comes in number 40 for general use and numbers 50 and 60 for fine fabrics and hand sewing. Use this thread for stitching cotton and linen fabrics.
Spun polyester thread is very strong and has more 'give', and should be used on stretch fabrics. It can also be used on wool fabrics.
Cotton-wrapped polyester thread has a coating of cotton around a polyester core; it is a strong thread, slightly thicker than polyester. Use it on all types of fabric except fine ones.
Pure silk thread is strong and lustrous and very good for hand sewing. Use silk thread on silk and wool fabrics.
Quilting thread is a lustrous, strong thread made of pure cotton or cotton-wrapped polyester. Because it does not tangle, it is ideal for most hand sewing.
Buttonhole twist is made from polyester or silk and is used for top stitching, for working hand-stitched buttonholes, and for sewing on buttons.

Pressing is a very important part of sewing. Each seam and dart should be pressed as soon as it is stitched to give it a clean, crisp finish. Your pressing equipment should always be ready to use when you are sewing.

THE IRON

The ideal iron for home-sewing purposes should be fairly heavy and capable of both dry and steam pressing. It should have a wide range of temperatures so that you can select the correct one for the fabric type. A spray for dampening stubborn creases is a useful extra feature.

THE IRONING BOARD

A sturdy, well made ironing board is essential. It should be adjustable so that it is a comfortable height for you to work at, and it should have a well padded cover that does not wrinkle. Add an extra layer of padding under the cover if it seems rather thin and flat.

TAILOR'S HAM

This is a firmly padded cushion with rounded ends which is used when pressing curved areas such as darts and curved seams. A pressing mitt serves the same function, but it is smaller and can be slipped over your hand or the tip of a sleeve board.

PRESS CLOTHS

Have a selection of clean white cloths for pressing. Use cheese-cloth for pressing lightweight fabrics and cotton or linen for heavier weights. Discard a press cloth as soon as it becomes discolored or scorched.

SLEEVE BOARD

A sleeve board looks like a miniature ironing board and is used on top of the normal board. It is designed for pressing narrow areas that will not thread onto an ironing board, so you are able to press a single layer of fabric at a time. A seam roll is a tightly packed cylindrical cushion that is used for pressing seams in the same restricted areas.

OPTIONAL EQUIPMENT

Other pressing aids are available and are useful if you intend to make tailored garments or work with heavy fabrics.

A wooden tailor's board has curves and straight edges and is used for precision pressing. A point presser is similar and is used for pressing corners and points. A tailor's clapper is a heavy block of wood used to pound creases into heavy fabric after it has been steamed. A needleboard that has a flat surface covered with steel wires is used for pressing pile fabrics; it will prevent the pile from being flattened when it is pressed. A pressing pad is composed of layers of soft fabric stitched together; it is used to press raised areas such as embroidered monograms so that they are not flattened.

Successful sewing depends to a great extent on the right choice of fabrics. This chapter provides a directory of the numerous fabrics available, giving details of how they are made, and what they are most suitable for. It suggests guidelines on judging the performance of different kinds of material and on how best to care for your fabrics.

Fabrics are made from different types of fibers which can be used singly or in combinations of two, three or more. These fibers may be natural, such as wool, linen, cotton, and silk, or man-made, such as acrylic, polyester and acetate. With the exception of silk, all natural fibers are short and are called staples. Silk and some synthetic fibers take the form of long, continuous strands called filaments. The staples and filament lengths are twisted into yarns, which are then made into a fabric. The appearance and durability of the yarn is affected by the degree of twist, with tightly twisted yarns being in general the smoothest and strongest.

Fabric is formed using one of a variety of techniques: weaving, knitting, felting or netting.

WEAVING

This is the most usual method of making fabric, in which two sets of yarns (the warp and the weft) are woven together to produce a fabric. The warp threads run lengthwise down the fabric, and they are crossed at right angles by the weft threads. The weave can be either plain or patterned, according to the arrangement of the threads.

KNITTING

Knitted fabric is stretchy and comfortable to wear. The fabric is formed by a series of interlocking loops. Weft-knitted fabric has the loops running crosswise and the stretch is greater across the fabric than down it. Warp-knitted fabric is made by forming the loops lengthwise and is more stable and durable than the weft-knitted type.

FELTING

Felted fabric is made from short lengths of fibers, usually wool or cotton, which are compressed and bonded together by heat and moisture. The fabric has no grain and is quite weak in wear. Wool felt will shrink if it is washed.

NETTING

Net is produced by machine to imitate a fabric which was originally hand made. The fabric has geometrically shaped holes outlined by yarn. The yarns are held together by knots where they intersect. Net can be extremely sheer, such as bridal tulle, or as heavy as fishnet, depending on the type of yarn that is used.

FABRIC CHOICE

COTTON AND LINEN

WOOL AND SILK

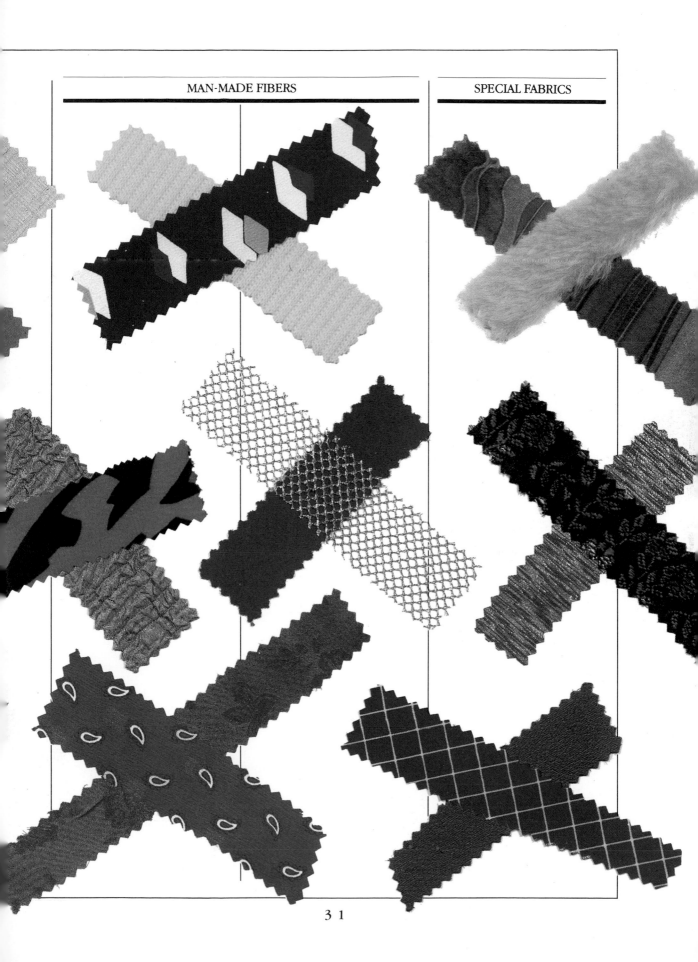

COTTON AND LINEN

Cotton is made from the fibers of the cotton plant. Plants grown in different areas of the world produce varying lengths and weights of fiber. The best quality cotton fabric is made with yarn spun from long, fine fibers such as Sea Island and Egyptian cotton. Cotton fabric is hard wearing, strong and absorbent, which makes it ideal for garments and home furnishings. Cotton does, however, crease in use and can shrink when it is washed. These problems can be overcome by special finishes or by the addition of a small amount of synthetic fibers.

Linen is made from the fibers that come from the stem of the flax plant. It is one of the oldest fibers in existence and, although expensive, it is extremely strong and hard wearing. Cotton is often added to linen for reasons of economy, and this mixture is an excellent fabric for heavy draperies and upholstery. Fabric made from linen is inclined to crease badly during use; the addition of synthetic fibers can prevent this.

Batiste A soft, sheer, lightweight fabric named after the French weaver, Jean Batiste. Made of cotton, linen, or a blend of the two, batiste may be used for summer dresses and shirts, baby clothes and lingerie.

Broadcloth A closely woven fabric similar in texture to fine poplin, made from cotton, synthetics, and blends; also, a woolen or worsted fabric with a lustrous finish and slight nap.

Brocade A fabric with areas of different weaves that create a raised pattern. Brocade can be cotton, synthetic, silk, or a blend.

Calico A lightweight, plain-weave cotton or cotton-blended fabric often printed with small floral patterns or other motifs. Calico originated in Calcutta, India.

Cambric A plain-weave fabric that is finished with a slightly glossy surface. Traditionally cambric is made from cotton or linen, but it can also be made from synthetics.

Canvas This term applies to several different fabrics, including cotton, linen, and synthetics. Canvas with a heavy, close weave is used for upholstery, sails, awnings, and tents and is also used in industry. The stiff open-weave mesh used for needlepoint is also called canvas. This term includes a linen fabric used as an interfacing in hand tailoring.

Chambray A cotton or cotton blend fabric in which the warp yarns are colored and the weft yarns are white. It is similar to denim but lighter weight. Chambray variations can include checks, stripes and small figured designs.

Chintz A glazed, medium-weight cotton fabric used for household accessories. Chintz is traditionally printed with a pattern of flowers and birds.

Corduroy A corded fabric in which the rib has been sheared after it is woven to produce a smooth, velvet-like nap. Traditionally made of cotton, corduroy can also be made from a cotton and synthetic blend which is crease resistant.

Damask Similar to brocade, damask has a flatter finish with a pattern produced by the contrast of areas of satin weave against a plain background. It is a popular fabric for tablecloths and napkins and can be made from cotton or linen.

Denim A twill-weave fabric usually made of cotton or cotton blend in which, traditionally, the warp yarns were dyed blue and the weft yarns were white.

Drill A sturdy, durable, twill-weave fabric of medium weight. Usually made of cotton or cotton blends, drill is used for garments and household accessories.

Eyelet A decorative embroidered fabric in which holes are cut or punched into a base fabric and the open areas surrounded by embroidery stitches. Originally hand stitched, eyelet is now made by machine. It is often used in narrow strips for edging garments. Although many different fabrics can be used as a base for the embroidery, white cotton and cotton blends are probably most common.

Gauze A sheer, lightweight fabric with a fairly open weave. In recent years handwoven cotton and cotton blend gauzes from India have been popular for both summer garments and curtains.

Gingham A firm, lightweight fabric made from cotton or cotton and polyester, with a woven pattern of regular checks.

Lace An open-work patterned fabric made either on a background fabric of net or without a background fabric. Lace can be made from cotton, nylon, viscose, silk or blends, and the patterns are usually floral in design. Modern lace is nearly always made by machine and many traditional hand-made lace patterns are copied. Lace is the traditional bridal fabric but is also used for other garments and for household items. Different types of lace include Brussels, Guipure, Nottingham, and Chantilly.

Lawn A fairly sheer, lightweight fabric made originally from linen but now usually made from combed cotton or blends of cotton and polyester. It can be solid color, printed, or have woven stripes.

Madras A hand-woven cotton fabric that originated in Madras, India. It is dyed in brilliant colors and often has a woven pattern of plaids, stripes, or checks. The dyes fade during washing to give the patterns a pleasantly muted coloring.

Muslin A plain-weave fabric usually woven from cotton or cotton blends. Muslin is made in a variety of weights, ranging from a sheer quality for light garments to a heavier fabric suitable for bedlinen. Unbleached muslin is used for interfacing.

Organdy Originally, organdy was a sheer cotton fabric with a stiff finish, and organza was the same fabric made of silk. These distinctions have now almost disappeared and the two names are sometimes synonymous. Organdy is also made from synthetics and blends of cotton and synthetic.

Piqué A fabric woven with small, raised ribs or geometric patterns. It is usually made from cotton or a blend of cotton and polyester. It is a crisp fabric that can be printed with colorful designs. White piqué is the classic fabric for tennis clothes and detachable collars and cuffs.

Plissé A puckered effect produced on cotton fabrics by shrinking some areas of the fabric with a chemical, caustic soda. The finish is reasonably permanent, but plissé fabrics should not be ironed, or the puckers will become flattened.

Poplin A light to medium-weight cotton with fine cross ribs formed by using a weft yarn which is thicker than the warp.

Ramie A fiber similar to linen but less expensive. It is often combined with cotton or polyester to make cool fabrics for summer wear.

Sateen A strong, satin-weave fabric made of cotton; it can be solid color or printed.

Seersucker A crinkled fabric made from cotton, cotton blends, or nylon. The crinkles are permanent and are not lost during laundering and wear.

Terry cloth An absorbent fabric made of cotton or blends of cotton and other fibers. It has uncut loops on one or both sides and is noted for its ability to absorb moisture. Terry cloth is used primarily for towels, but it is also used for garments.

Voile A light, delicate cotton or silk fabric used for summer garments and lightweight curtains.

WOOL AND SILK

Wool fabrics are made from yarn spun from the fleece of sheep. It is hard wearing, soft and absorbent, and has good insulating properties. Wool yarns come in two distinct types: woolen and worsted. Woolen yarns are generally made from shorter fibers. Worsted yarns are smoother and are made from longer fibers. Other types of wool fabrics are made from the coats of goats, rabbits and camels.

Silk is a fine and expensive natural fiber produced from the cocoon of the silkworm. It is soft and extremely strong, as well as attractive in appearance.

Alpaca A South American goat-like animal gives its name to the wool that comes from its fleece. Fabric woven from alpaca fibers is soft, warm, and silky. Alpaca fibers can be blended with cotton, wool or viscose.

Angora Long, silky fibers from the coat of the angora rabbit, which are blended with wool or synthetics to make a soft, fluffy fabric.

Barathea A fine, closely woven, smooth wool fabric with a broken rib pattern.

Bouclé A rough, looped wool fabric with a textured, nubby surface that is usually dull unless a shiny synthetic fiber is added.

Camel hair A fiber that is obtained from the underhair of the Bactrian camel. The fiber is light brown in color and because the color cannot be removed easily, camel hair fabrics are generally found in natural or dark colors. The fabric is lustrous, soft, but not very hard wearing. Camel hair is often blended with sheep's wool to add durability.

Cashmere A soft, luxurious, warm fiber from the underhair of the cashmere goat, which is made into an attractive fabric. Cashmere fabric is not hard wearing.

Challis A soft, lightweight, plain-weave fabric originally made of worsted wool but now also made from synthetic fibers. Challis is frequently printed in small floral or paisley patterns.

Crepe A fabric with a nubby, crinkly surface made from wool, silk or synthetic fibers.

Flannel A plain or twill-weave fabric of medium-weight with a napped finish, usually made of wool or cotton.

Foulard A lightweight fabric in a plain or twill weave, originally made from silk, now also made from synthetics. Foulard is often printed with small patterns on solid color backgrounds.

Gabardine A wool or cotton fabric which has a close, firm, twill weave.

Harris tweed A woolen tweed which is handwoven from yarns spun on the islands of the Outer Hebrides off the coast of Scotland. The yarns may be spun by hand or machine.

Herringbone A twill-weave woolen fabric in which the warp and weft yarns interlace to produce a pattern resembling the backbone of the herring fish.

Honan A type of silk fabric woven from raw silk, originally made in the Honan region of China. Raw silk is more uneven and coarse than cultivated silk and the fabric has an interesting texture.

Irish Tweed A woolen tweed that is usually made with a white warp and colored weft.

Llama Hair from the fleece of this South American animal is often used alone or blended with wool to make a fine and lustrous fabric. The natural colors of llama hair are predominantly black or brown.

Mohair Fiber from the angora goat which is lustrous, smooth and hard wearing. Mohair fiber is often blended with wool and other fibers.

Pongee A light or medium-weight silk fabric made from raw silk; it is available in a wide range of colors.

Raw silk The silk from uncultivated silkworms; it is rougher and more uneven than cultivated silk. The fabric is usually duller in finish and rougher in texture than other types of silk.

Satin One of the basic weaves of silk fabrics. Silk satin is expensive so the fabric is now imitated using various synthetic fibers. Types of fabrics include antique, double faced, duchesse, and slipper satin

Serge A durable fabric with a close, twill weave. At one time serge was always made of worsted wool, but it is now made in a variety of synthetic fibers also.

Shantung A fabric originally made from silk, but now also of cotton and synthetic fibers. The yarn is slubbed and irregular, giving a nubby texture.

Spun silk A medium-weight, inexpensive matte silk. The yarn from which spun silk is woven is made from short, waste lengths of silk filament.

Tartan A plaid pattern associated with a specific Scottish family or area group, called a clan. Tartan fabrics are usually made from wool and occasionally from cotton.

Thai silk An iridescent silk fabric, made in Thailand; it is often slubbed and dyed in vivid colors.

Tussah A heavy, raw silk fabric with an attractive, uneven weave.

Tweed A hard-wearing, woven fabric characterized by colored slubs of yarn on a hairy surface. Tweed may be made of any fiber combination, although wool tweed is probably the most common.

Vicuna A fiber from the coat of the vicuna, a wild animal that lives in the Andes mountains. Although some vicuna have been domesticated, the animal is found mostly in the wild and must be killed to obtain the hair which is one of the softest, finest fibers known; the hair is spun and woven into an expensive fabric. The fibers are difficult to dye, and the fabric is usually found in the natural color, a light tan to chestnut brown.

Woolen A fabric made from wool fibers which have been carded before they are spun. A woolen fabric is rough, hairy, and fairly hard wearing.

Worsted A type of wool fabric or yarn. Worsted fabrics are made from yarns that have been combed as well as carded. Worsted yarns are smoother than woolen yarns and make a hard-wearing fabric with a clean, smooth surface as contrasted with the hairy surface of woolens.

FABRIC DIRECTORY

MAN-MADE FIBERS

Man-made fibers Man-made fibers are the twentieth-century addition to the range of natural fibers used to make yarns and fabrics.

These fibers include those made from a natural substance, such as acetate, as well as synthetics made from chemicals. Synthetics are cheap to produce and have easy care properties, unlike many of the natural fibers, which crease and shrink badly and need careful laundering. However, they are less comfortable to wear and most of them lack the distinctive appearance of wool, silk, linen, and cotton. Many modern fabrics are made from blends of natural and synthetic fibers to give the best of both worlds.

Acetate Acetate is a cellulose-based fiber which has been available since 1918. It is made from dissolved cotton fibers or wood shavings. The result is extruded to form a yarn which is soft, silky, and moth and mildew resistant. Acetate is used to make imitation silk fabrics and is also blended with silk and cotton.

Acrylic Acrylic yarns have been available since the early 1950s; they are warmer than the other synthetics such as nylon and polyester. Acrylic fabrics are often an imitation of wool fabrics, and they are light, soft, and crease resistant.

Modacrylic A modified version of acrylic fibers which is almost completely flame resistant.

Modal Modal is a cellulose-based fiber which is very similar to cotton, but more absorbent. It is often blended with cotton or polyester to produce an inexpensive, comfortable fabric suitable for garments.

Nylon This fiber is also known as polyamide and it has been available since 1938. Either a filament or staple yarn, it is strong, lightweight, washes well and dries quickly. Nylon yarns do not crease and they are resistant to moth and mildew. The fibers mix well with others and they are used in a variety of fabrics.

Polyester Polyester is a versatile fiber that can be spun and woven to imitate silk, cotton, wool or linen. It is crease resistant, easy to care for and hard wearing, and it is often blended with cotton to add these properties to a fabric.

Rayon Rayon was the first man-made fiber to be produced on a large scale, and it has been available since 1910. Its use declined after World War II when people wanted the polyesters and nylons that did not wrinkle or need ironing, but it has recently made a comeback in a new form, which is more versatile and easily washable.

Rayon is made of cellulose from pine, hemlock and spruce trees. Today it is usually blended with other fibers, because it does not wear well when used alone. It absorbs moisture and breathes nearly as easily as cotton (the cellular structure of cotton and rayon are virtually the same), yet is a more flowing, more sensuously clingy material. However, it is not nearly as strong as cotton, linen, silk or wool, and should not be bought for anything from which sturdy wear is desired. Most of the newer rayons can be handwashed and ironed with a warm iron, but never iron rayon with a hot iron as it will burn.

Special fabrics include velvets, fur and fur fabric, knits and leather.

Astrakhan cloth A heavy woven or knitted fabric with a curly pile which imitates the natural fur, Persian lamb.

Batting Batting is a thick layer of compressed polyester or cotton fibers that is used in quilting.

Candlewick A thick, soft yarn used to form tufts by pulling it through a base fabric and then cutting it. The term also describes the fabric made with this yarn that is used to make bedspreads and throw pillows.

Double cloth Reversible fabrics made with three to five sets of yarns. Some doublecloth fabrics appear the same on both sides, some have a reversed pattern, and others are different on each side, depending on the techniques used for weaving the fabric.

Double knit A knitted fabric which has one knit stitch directly behind another, so that the fabric is the same on both sides.

Fake fur A fabric which imitates animal pelts. The most popular fake furs are made from modacrylic fiber.

Felt A non-woven wool fabric made from fibers that have been joined through the natural felting qualities of the fiber. Wool and some other animal hair fibers felt naturally when subjected to the application of heat, moisture, and pressure. Felt is mainly used as a decoration, as it is weak and tears easily.

Flocked fabric A fabric to which short fibers have been attached with an adhesive. Flocked fabrics can be made to simulate materials such as suede and velvet. The fibers can be applied over all the fabric surface or in selected areas to form patterns.

Fur Fur is the coat of an animal which is used in the same ways as fabric. Types of fur include rabbit, mink, fox, sable, sheepskin, and chinchilla.

Fusible fabric A fabric which can be joined to another fabric in a fairly permanent bond through the application of heat, moisture, and pressure.

Interfacing A layer of fabric placed under the main fabric to support and strengthen it. Interfacing can be either sewn in or fused to the main fabric.

Interlining An extra layer of fabric in a garment that is intended to provide additional warmth or support a loosely woven fabric.

Jacquard knit A knitted fabric with the design knitted into the fabric in a regular all-over pattern.

Lamé A fabric woven or knitted with all metallic yarns or with a combination of metallic and other fiber yarns.

Leather The hide of an animal with the fur removed or the skin of a reptile. Leather has been used throughout history for clothing and other purposes. Today, synthetic fabrics which imitate leather are widely available. Common leather types include alligator, buckskin, calfskin, chamois, cowhide, crocodile, kid, lambskin, morocco, patent, pigskin, snakeskin, and suede.

Lining A layer of fabric that gives a neat finish to the inside of an article. Lining fabrics are made from inexpensive types of silk or man-made fibers.

Net A fabric which is constructed by knotting and looping a continuous yarn to form an open mesh.

Pattern knit A knitted fabric made by dropping, adding, rearranging, and crossing various stitches to create intricate designs.

Plain or single knit A flat-surfaced knitted fabric with a smooth face and looped reverse.

Raschel knit A knitted fabric which imitates crochet or net.

Rib knit A knitted fabric which consists of groups of alternate plain and purl stitches.

Tulle A very fine net made originally from silk and now made from nylon.

Velvet A fabric with a short, closely woven pile made from silk and synthetics. There are two methods of making velvet. One method uses a double cloth construction, in which two layers of fabric are woven with long threads joining them. After weaving, the joining threads are cut, producing two pieces of velvet. In the other weaving process, the yarn is lifted over wires to form the pile. When the wires are removed, the yarn is cut to form the pile.

Velveteen A cotton fabric with a short pile, similar to velvet.

FABRIC FINISHES

The handle and performance of a fabric can be changed by the addition of a special finish. Check the label on the fabric you buy to see if it has a finish and whether there are any special fabric care instructions. The most common fabric finishes are described below.

Colorfast The dyes used on the fabric will not run during washing provided the fabric care instructions are followed. This finish will also prevent colors from fading in direct sunlight.

Crease resistant The fabric has been treated so that it will shed creases. This finish does not mean that creasing will be totally prevented.

Flame resistant The fabric has been treated so that it will not burn once the source of the fire has been removed. This is especially important when choosing fabric for making nightwear and children's clothes.

Mercerized This finish is found on cotton fabrics and sewing threads. It strengthens the fibers and gives them a slight sheen.

Mothproof This finish is found on wool and silk fabrics that are prone to damage by moth larvae.

Pre-shrunk The fabric has been shrunk during manufacture and will not shrink more than one or two per cent during laundering.

Stain repellent This finish is found mainly on furnishing fabrics and means that the fabric has been treated to resist staining.

Wash and wear The fabric has been treated so that it can be washed and worn without requiring ironing. Repeated washing will eventually destroy the finish.

Water repellent This finish reduces the water absorption of fibers and is found on cotton and nylon fabrics. This finish does not mean that the fabric is totally waterproof.

CHOOSING FABRICS

Successful sewing depends to a great extent on the right choice of fabrics. The color and pattern of the fabric is, of course, largely a matter of personal preference and the amount of money available, but the following points should also be taken into consideration.

When choosing fabric for a garment, stand in front of a mirror and drape the fabric in front of you. Check that it will suit your coloring and that the weight of the fabric is suitable for the style of garment that you have in mind.

When choosing fabric to make into an item for the home, take color samples of your existing fabrics, wallpaper, and paint to check that the color match or contrast will work well.

Crush a corner of the fabric in your hand and see whether it will spring back into shape without creasing badly.

Check the raw edges of the fabric for excessive fraying. If your chosen fabric does fray badly, allow ¼inch (5mm) extra on the seam allowances when cutting out.

Pull knit fabrics gently lengthwise and widthwise to check the "give". Make sure that the fabric springs back into its original shape after stretching.

Look at the pattern or weave to see if the fabric has a "one way" pattern or a nap. You may need to buy extra fabric if this is the case.

Check the straightness of the grain.

Unroll some of the fabric and check if there are any flaws.

Check the fiber composition of the fabric and whether there are any special finishes and cleaning instructions.

Launder fabric items carefully to make sure that they last as long as possible. Follow any instructions given when the fabric was purchased and dry clean if the washability is in doubt. Clean fabric items before they become really dirty; otherwise the dirt may become ingrained and difficult to remove. This is especially important for white and pastel colored fabrics and for synthetics, which tend to hold the dirt.

INTERNATIONAL CARE SYMBOLS

Garments made in Europe bear labels giving washing and dry cleaning information in the form of a series of symbols.
The five main symbols for washing, bleaching, dry cleaning, ironing, and drying are shown below. A cross through any of these symbols means "do not use".
① This symbol represents the washing process and all instructions relating to it.
② The triangle represents chlorine bleaching instructions.
③ The iron represents ironing instructions including temperatures, which are indicated by dots inside the symbol. One dot indicates the temperature for man-made fabrics, two dots are for polyester blends, silk, and wool, and three dots are for cotton, linen, and viscose.
④ The circle represents dry cleaning and the type of solvent that should be used.
⑤ This symbol represents tumble drying, which may be either harmful or beneficial for some fabrics.

WASHING SYMBOLS

These symbols give a reliable temperature guide for washing fabrics.

① White cotton and linen articles without special finishes.

② Cotton, linen, and viscose articles. No special finishes: colors fast at 140°F(60°C).

③ White nylon, white polyester, and cotton blends.

④ Colored nylon, cotton, and viscose blends with special finishes, colored polyester/cotton blends.

⑤ Cotton, linen, and viscose articles where colors are fast at 40°F (5°C), but not at 60°F (15°C).

⑥ Acrylic, acetate, and triacetate, including blends with wool, polyester, and wool blends.

⑦ Wool, wool blends with cotton or viscose, silk.

⑧ Silk and printed acetate fabrics with colors not fast at 40°F (5°C).

⑨ Cotton articles with special finishes which can be boiled but require drip drying.

⑩ Hand wash only.

This chapter explains the different sewing methods that are used to make garments and accessories for the home. The first section deals with hand-sewing – an important addition to the sewing machine techniques described in Chapter 1. The later sections take you through the constructional elements of sewing: seams, hems, shaping, and fastenings.

Most garments and items for the home are made initially on the machine and then finished by hand. Hand finishing should be neat and unobtrusive, so take care to use the correct stitch for the job in hand; otherwise the results could be disappointing. If you are not familiar with some of the stitches shown, take time to practice them on a scrap of fabric until you feel confident with your technique. Never try to hurry hand sewing – it should be an enjoyable and relaxed process. The size needle to use when sewing by hand is largely a matter of personal preference, but a fine needle will generally give a neater result.

STARTING TO SEW

Good light is essential when sewing. Sit in a comfortable chair where there is good natural light, or use a directional lamp. Assemble the equipment you will need before you begin sewing and keep it together within easy reach. Make sure that your hands are scrupulously clean and try to use a thimble to prevent wear and tear on the fingers. When sewing white fabrics, shake some talcum powder on your hands to help prevent the fabric from becoming fingermarked.

Use a small knot at the end of the thread unless you are working on a fine, delicate fabric, when a few tiny stitches should be used to secure the end. Hide the knot under a fold or at the edge of the fabric if the stitching is to be permanent. Keep the length of working thread fairly short to prevent it from tangling. Fasten off the thread with two or three backstitches, again hiding them under a fold or at the edge of the fabric.

Keeping the correct tension when hand sewing is just as important as when you are using a machine. It should be correct for the fabric — if it is too tight, puckers and wrinkles will occur. When stitching is loose, the layers of fabric will part and the stitching could eventually break. The secret of even tension is practice and familiarity with the particular stitch you are using.

BASTING

Basting is used to keep layers of fabric together temporarily after pinning and before machine stitching. Use a thread that contrasts well with the fabric to make the basting easy to remove. The stitches should be between ¼ inch (5mm) and ⅜ inch (1cm) long.

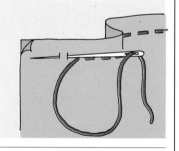

UNEVEN BASTING STITCH

Uneven basting is also used to hold layers of fabric together, but although it is quicker, it is not as strong as the previous stitch. Take long stitches on one side of the fabric and short stitches on the reverse.

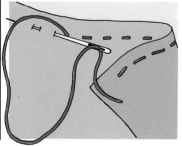

DIAGONAL BASTING STITCH

Diagonal basting is used to hold layers of fabric firmly together within an area. It keeps the fabric flat where a row of ordinary basting could cause a ridge — for example, when attaching interfacing or holding a pleat in place. Take horizontal stitches from right to left through the fabric as shown to leave a row of diagonal stitches on the right side.

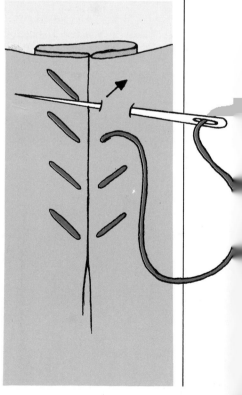

RUNNING STITCH

Running stitch is used mainly for gathering and shirring fabric. It is basically the same as basting, but smaller, and the stitches must be even. Take several small stitches on the point of the needle before pulling it through the fabric. When gathering fabric, make sure that the thread is long enough to make an unbroken line of stitching.

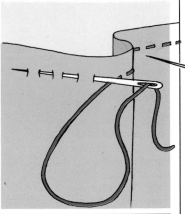

HALF BACKSTITCH

Half backstitch is similar to ordinary backstitch but a longer stitch is taken on the reverse of the fabric, which spaces out the stitches on the front. From the front, the stitches should form a neat, broken line. When the stitches on the front are very tiny, this stitch is known as prick stitch.

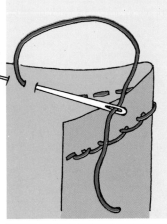

WHIP STITCH

Whip stitch is used instead of slipstitch to join two folded edges of fabric when a strong joining is needed. Work from right to left as shown taking a small amount of fabric from each fold. Pull the sewing thread quite tightly to give a neat joining.

BACKSTITCH

Backstitch is a strong stitch which can be used to make a garment if a machine is not available. It is also used to stitch parts of a garment that are awkward to reach with a machine. The stitches on the front of the work look like machine stitches, and they should be small and worked perfectly evenly. Two or three backstitches worked on top of each other can also be used to start and finish hand stitching.

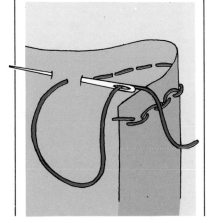

OVERCASTING

Overcasting is used to finish the edges of fabrics that fray easily. Work from either direction, taking the thread over the edge of the fabric. Do not pull the thread too tightly, or the edges of the fabric will curl and make bulges. If the fabric frays badly, work a row of machine stitching first and trim the fabric close to this stitching before overcasting over the edge and the machine stitching.

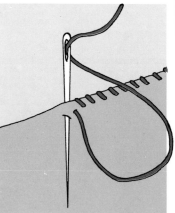

PRICK STITCH

Prick stitch is a small, strong stitch worked through several layers of fabric. It is a good stitch to use when attaching a zipper by hand as it is almost invisible on the right side. Prick stitch looks similar to half backstitch, but it is worked with a stabbing motion through the fabric layers. Work prick stitch from the right side, since it is untidy on the reverse side.

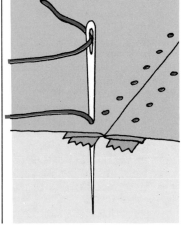

BLANKET STITCH

Blanket stitch is a looped stitch used mainly for finishing raw edges. The loops can be close together or spaced apart, depending on where the stitch is used. Open blanket stitch, with the stitches set widely apart, is also used as an alternative to herringbone stitch for finishing edges and holding them down. Close blanket stitch is used over bar tacks and button shanks.

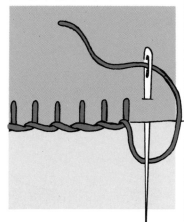

HEMMING STITCH

Hemming stitch is used to hold down the fold of a hem on light and medium-weight fabrics. This stitch may show on the right side. The thread should not be pulled taut or the fabric may pucker. Work toward yourself, picking up a thread of the single fabric and then a thread of the fold before pulling the needle through.

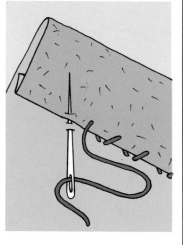

SLIPSTITCH

Slipstitch is used to join two folded edges of fabric or a folded edge to a layer of flat fabric. If worked carefully, it should be almost invisible. It can be worked from the right side which makes it especially useful for finishing the ends of ties, waistbands and cuffs. Pull the thread just enough to join the folds securely; the fabric will wrinkle if the tension is too tight. Slipstitch is also used to finish hems on fine, delicate fabrics.

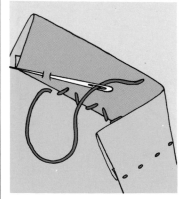

TAILOR'S BUTTONHOLE STITCH

This stitch is used for working buttonholes in preference to close blanket stitch, since it is stronger and more hard wearing. Worked in a similar way, it forms a row of knots against the raw edge. Always keep the stitches close together and make sure that the knots touch in order to keep the edge firm.

BLIND STITCH

Blind stitch is worked on the inside fold of a hem and worked from right to left. The stitches are almost invisible, provided the thread is not pulled tightly, which makes it ideal for skirt or dress hems. This stitch can also be used to hold down a fold of fabric which has had the raw edge finished by overcasting or by zigzag stitch.

HERRINGBONE STITCH

Although primarily an embroidery stitch, herringbone stitch is used in hand sewing for securing hems on heavy fabrics. Work it directly over the raw edge; the edge will be finished at the same time. Herringbone stitch is fairly elastic, so it is ideal for use with stretch fabrics and knits.

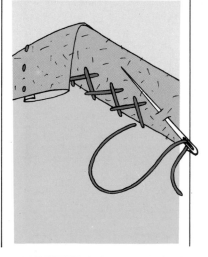

TAILOR'S TACKS

Tailor's tacks are the most accurate method of transferring markings from a paper pattern to double layers of fabric. Use them to mark seamlines, darts, and other construction symbols and also to mark delicate fabrics, which may be damaged by using other methods such as a tracing wheel. Always leave the pattern pinned to the fabric until all marks have been transferred from it. With the point of the needle, slit the pattern across the symbol to be marked before working the tailor's tack and always use double thread. Take care not to pull the tacks out when lifting the pattern off the fabric. After the pattern has been removed, gently separate the layers of fabric and cut the loops with sharp scissors.

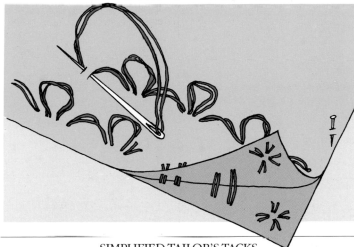

SIMPLIFIED TAILOR'S TACKS

Simplified tailor's tacks are used to mark a line of pleats or a seamline on a single piece of fabric. They consist of a continuous row of loose stitches in double thread as shown. Cut the thread between each stitch before carefully removing the pattern, taking care not to pull out the markings.

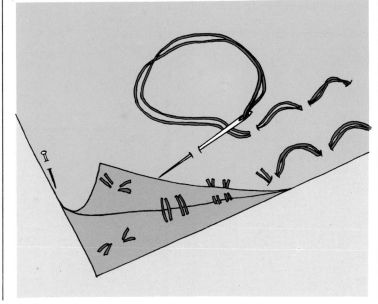

FELLING STITCH

Felling stitch is used in tailoring to attach loose linings to the neckline, seams, and front edges of coats and jackets. Baste the lining in position with the raw edge folded under, and work with this fold away from you as shown. The stitches should be neat, tiny, and almost invisible. The joining made will be extremely strong.

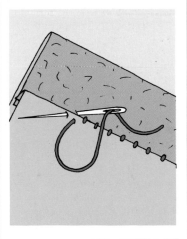

BAR TACK

A bar tack is a strengthening device used to prevent fabric from tearing, for example, at the base of a zipper or across the end of a sleeve opening. A bar of straight stitches is worked through the fabric first. Closely spaced blanket stitches are then worked over this bar without the needle penetrating the fabric. Take care to fasten off the thread securely on the wrong side of the fabric.

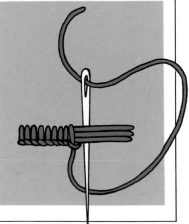

P L A I N   S E A M S

Seams are formed when two or more pieces of fabric are joined together by a line of stitching. They are the main constructional element in sewing, and should be worked with care. Seams are usually machine stitched, but they can be sewn by hand using backstitch.

Plain seams create the shape of a garment or household accessory and should be almost invisible when pressed. Decorative seams emphasize the lines of shaping and are often used as a strong design feature. The choice of seam will also depend on the weight of the fabric and the type of article being made. For example, a flat fell seam used on denim jeans will be more durable and suitable for repeated laundering than a flat seam.

FLAT SEAM

A flat seam is the basic method used to join fabrics of average weight. It is always sewn with the right sides of the fabric facing, and the raw edges should be finished to prevent fraying. Finish straight flat seams after stitching and pressing open. A plain straight stitch should be used on woven fabric, with the appropriate sizes of needle and thread.

Stretch fabric needs to be sewn with a stitch that allows the seam to "give," otherwise the stitching will break during use. A small straight stitch and polyester thread will often give sufficient stretch, or a very narrow zigzag stitch can be used. Some machines have a special stretch stitch; use this with care, for it is difficult to rip out. A flat zigzag seam will need to be pressed to one side to accommodate the width of the stitching.

① Place the two pieces of fabric together with right sides facing and edges even, and pin and baste along the seamline.

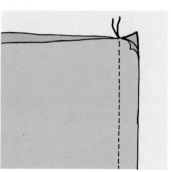

② Machine stitch along the seamline. Remove basting, and press.

CROSSED SEAM

A crossed seam is formed when two pieces of fabric that each contain a flat seam are joined at right angles to the seams.
① Finish the raw edges of the seams before joining the pieces together. Placing the right sides of the two pieces of fabric together, pin along the seamline, making sure that the crossed seams align by inserting a fine pin through both seams as shown.

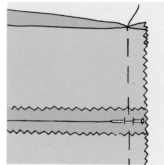

② After basting and stitching the seam, trim the seam allowances diagonally to reduce any bulk. Remove the basting and press the seam open.

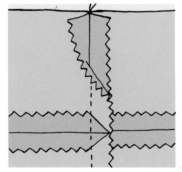

FRENCH SEAM

A French seam is a narrow seam which encloses the raw edges of the fabric so that fraying does not occur. It is normally used on fine, semi-transparent fabric or on medium-weight fabric that has a tendency to fray badly. Do not use this seam on heavy fabrics, for the effect will be bulky and unsightly. This seam is often used on baby clothes and lingerie. The finished seam should be no wider than $\frac{1}{4}$ inch (5mm). It is always pressed to one side, toward the back of the garment.
① Place the two pieces of fabric together with wrong sides facing. Pin, baste and stitch about $\frac{3}{8}$ inch (1cm) from the raw edges. Trim both the seam allowances to $\frac{1}{8}$ inch (3mm).

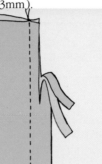

② Refold so that the right sides are together and the seam is at the edge. Pin, baste and stitch along the seam again, this time $\frac{1}{4}$ inch (5mm) from the edge.

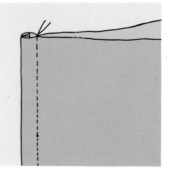

FLAT FELL SEAM

A flat fell seam is a very useful self-finishing seam which is used extensively where a strong, non-fraying seam is needed. Use this seam on medium-weight fabrics such as poplin and challis, since it is rather bulky when used on heavy fabrics. Two rows of stitching show on one side of the seams, these can be in contrasting colors. Denim jeans are usually put together using flat fell seams, because they are durable.
① Place the two pieces of fabric with wrong sides facing. Pin, baste and stitch about $\frac{5}{8}$ inch (1.5cm) from the raw edges. Trim one seam allowance to $\frac{1}{4}$ inch (5mm).

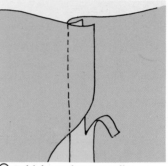

② Fold the wider seam allowance in half with the raw edge to the seamline. The narrower seam allowance is now neatly enclosed. Press the seam down flat and then baste to keep the folded edge in place. Stitch along the fold to finish.

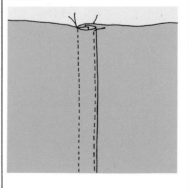

P L A I N   S E A M S

TAPED SEAM

A taped seam is similar to a flat seam, but it is used on areas that will be subjected to strain, especially on garments. It incorporates seam binding or tape, which should always be preshrunk to prevent the seam from puckering after it is laundered.

① Place the two pieces of fabric together with right sides facing, and pin and baste along the seamline. Baste a length of seam binding or tape along the seamline. If you are taping a curved seam, ease the binding or tape carefully around the curve while you are basting it.

② Turn the fabric over with the taped side facing down, and stitch close to the basting. Remove basting before pressing.

SELF-BOUND SEAM

This seam is used where one piece of fabric is gathered and one is flat. It is also useful for fraying fabrics, since the raw edges are enclosed, but it forms a rather bulky ridge and is only successful on lightweight fabrics.

① Place the two pieces of fabric together with right sides facing, with the gathered piece on top. Baste along the seamline and stitch. Remove basting; trim upper or gathered seam allowance only to ¼ inch (5mm).

② Fold the wider edge over twice, bringing it over to meet the line of stitching. Baste and press.

③ For a soft finish to the seam, hand-sew the fold, taking the stitches into the machine-stitched line, rather than through the fabric. Alternatively, machine stitch along close to the fold. This will give a harder ridge, but it will be more hard wearing.

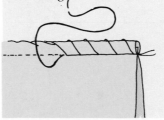

④ When using this seam on flimsy fabric, make the seam narrower by trimming the wider seam allowance to ¼ inch (5mm), and the narrower one to about 1/16 inch (2mm). Fold down as in step 2, and overcast over the edge, bringing the needle through just above the line of stitching and pulling the stitches fairly tight.

CURVED SEAM

A curved seam is used to provide shaping. It is used to join two pieces of fabric that differ in shape, for one piece will generally be more curved than the other.

① Place the two pieces of fabric together with right sides facing, with the more curved piece on top. Pin them together exactly on the seamline with the points of the pins facing outward as shown, picking up a tiny piece of fabric each time. Ease the top piece into position and hold the seam over your hand to pin, keeping the curve even.

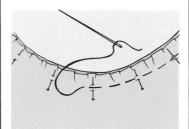

② Baste along the seamline with small stitches and remove the pins. If the fabric is quite stiff, you will need to clip the seam allowance as you work.

③ Keeping the more shaped piece on top, stitch carefully along the curve, following the basted line closely. Trim seam allowance and clip further if necessary. Either press this seam open and finish the edges separately, or press it to one side and finish the edges together.

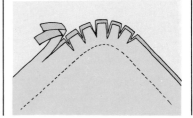

CORNER SEAM

A corner seam is used to provide shaping and is usually constructed using an ordinary flat seam. This seam is a little tricky, for it is difficult to keep the corner sharp and neat. If the seam will not be enclosed, finish the edges of the fabric before beginning the seam.
① Mark the corner points on the fabric with tailor's tacks. Placing the right sides of the two pieces of fabric together, pin along one side up to the corner inserting the pins at right angles to the seamline.

② Clip the top piece of fabric at the corner point. Stitch the pinned seam to the corner, leaving the point of the needle in the fabric.

③ Pivot the work around the needle. Align both layers of fabric as shown, then pin the second side of the seam and stitch to the end. Remove the tailor's tacks and press the seam flat.

WELT SEAM

A welt seam is extremely strong and is suitable for use on almost all fabrics, apart from fine fabrics, which have a tendency to fray badly. A row of stitching shows on the right side. This can add interest to a solid-color fabric if a contrasting thread is used.
① Place the two pieces of fabric together with right sides facing. Pin, baste and stitch along the seamline. Remove the basting and press the seam to one side, depending on where you want the row of stitching to show.
② Open the pressed seam allowances and trim the lower one to slightly less than $3/8$ inch (1cm). At this stage, finish the edge of the wider seam allowance unless the item is to be lined.

③ Turn the fabric right side up and baste parallel to the seamline, basting through the wider seam allowance as shown. The narrow seam allowance is now enclosed. Stitch or topstitch with a heavier thread from the right side, keeping the line of stitching parallel to the original seam and inside the line of basting. Press the seam again from the right side.

NARROW FINISH SEAM

A narrow finish seam is used only on lightweight or semi-transparent fabrics. It is an inconspicuous way of joining fine fabrics and can be finished by hand or machine.

① Place the two pieces of fabric together with the right sides facing. Pin, baste and stitch along the seamline. Remove the basting and press the seam to one side.

② To finish by machine, trim the seam allowances to ¼ inch (5mm) and zigzag over both together.

③ To finish by hand, fold the seam allowances in to meet each other, as shown. Baste the folds together, press, and slipstitch neatly.

ROLLED SEAM

A rolled seam is used on fine fabrics and is a self-finishing seam. It looks rather similar to a French seam, but only one row of stitching is used. Use rolled seams on loosely fitting garments only, as they could split when stretched.

① Place the two pieces of fabric together with the right sides facing and baste along the seamline. Trim one seam allowance to within ⅛ inch (3mm) of the basting. On a very fine fabric, also trim the wider allowance slightly.

② Fold the wider seam allowance over once, and then fold it just over the basted line. Baste through the fold along the seamline. Stitch along the edge of the fold, remove basting, and press from the wrong side.

CHANNEL OR SLOT SEAM

A channel seam can be used on most types of fabric, but it will work best on a solid-color, fairly firm fabric. It incorporates a backing strip which shows between the seam edges. This can be cut from a matching, contrasting, or patterned fabric. Try to use the same weight of fabric for the backing strip as for the main item, or back a finer fabric with iron-on interfacing for added firmness. The width of the backing strip depends on the weight of the fabric and how much of it will be seen. Usually, the maximum amount that should show through is $\frac{1}{4}$ inch (5mm), but it could be larger to give a more decorative effect.

When adding this type of seam to a pattern piece, join the seam first, using larger pieces of fabric, and then cut out the complete section, using the pattern.

① Turn in the raw edges of the two pieces of main fabric along the seamline. Baste, press and finish the edges. Cut a bias strip of the contrasting fabric at least 1$\frac{1}{4}$ inch (3cm) wide. Finish the edges and mark the center of the strip with a line of basting.

② Baste one folded edge of the main fabric, right side up, to the strip, about $\frac{1}{16}$ inch (2mm) from the center. The top edge of the main fabric should be slightly lower than the edge of the backing strip, as shown. Baste the other folded edge in the same way, keeping both folds parallel. Work a row of diagonal basting across the folds as shown.

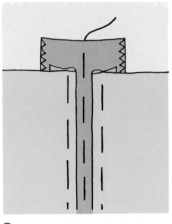

③ On the right side, stitch along the folds about $\frac{1}{8}$ inch (3mm) away from the edge. Remove the basting and press from the wrong side on a well-padded surface.

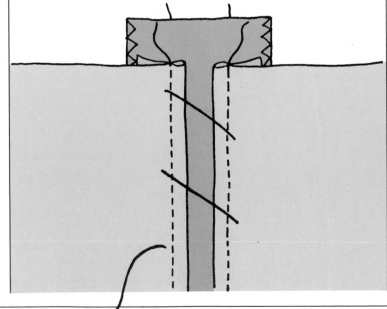

TOPSTITCHED SEAM

A plain flat seam can be decorated by topstitching it in a matching or contrasting color, or heavier weight of thread. The stitching can be on one side of the seam or both, and can be worked by hand or machine. Decorative machine stitches can also be used. Check the size of the seam allowance before you begin cutting out, and add a little extra if necessary. If you are topstitching along both sides of the seam, always stitch in the same direction or the stitching could pull the fabric and make it pucker.

① Make a flat seam, press, and finish the edges. Baste through the layers of fabric at the chosen distance from the seam, and stitch on the right side close to the basted lines as shown. Remove the basting and press.

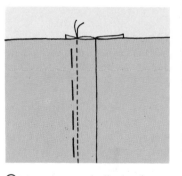

② To give a raised effect to the seam, cut narrow bias strips of fine fabric and insert them under the seam allowance on the wrong side. Finish the seam as above.

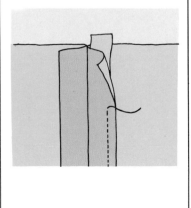

INSERTION SEAM

An insertion seam is used to attach lengths of lace or braid to lingerie and garments made from lightweight fabrics. The insertions can be made almost anywhere on the garment and can be as wide or narrow as you like. They are added after the pattern pieces have been cut out, since no extra seam allowance is needed.

① Mark the position of the insertion on the right side of the main fabric, using a line of basting or tailor's tacks. Place one edge of the insertion along the markings and baste it in place. Holding the insertion flat to prevent puckering, baste it down along the second side.

② Attach the insertion on the right side with straight, zigzag, or machine embroidery stitches. Use a matching thread so the stitching is inconspicuous and keep the stitching as close to the edge as possible. Remove the basting, then press from the wrong side on a well-padded surface.

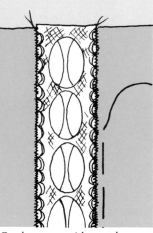

③ On the wrong side, cut the fabric away between the rows of stitching, using a sharp pair of scissors. Trim the edges and finish them with overcasting. When using a transparent insertion, roll the edges back to the main fabric and hand hem. This will prevent them from showing through on the right side and spoiling the look of the finished garment.

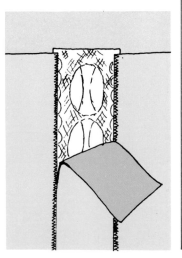

LAPPED SEAM

A lapped seam is simple to construct and relies on the use of a contrasting thread to add decoration. One side of the seam laps over the other. This seam can be used on any type of fabric.

① After deciding which way the seam will face, turn under the seam allowance on the top layer of fabric along the seamline. Baste along the fold and press. Place this on the other piece of fabric with the right sides uppermost, matching the seamlines, and baste in place.

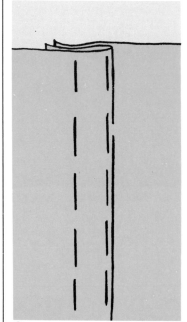

② Stitch along the fold on the right side using a straight, zigzag, or machine embroidery stitch and a contrasting thread; take care to keep the line of stitching perfectly even.

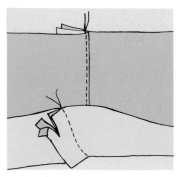

FAGOTED SEAM

A fagoted seam is very decorative but not particularly strong, so avoid using this seam on garments that are going to be worn frequently. The two pieces of fabric are joined with hand embroidery, leaving a small gap between them. The gap can vary between ⅛ inch (3mm) on fine fabric and ⅜ inch (1cm) on wool or heavy cottons. Work a fagoted seam on a larger piece of fabric first and then cut out the pattern pieces.

① Mark the position of the fagoting on the right side of the fabric with a line of basting. Cut the fabric on this line and press a narrow double hem to the wrong side along each edge. Hand-hem each piece.

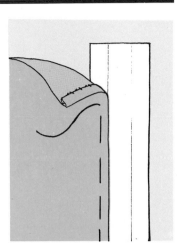

② With a pencil and ruler, mark parallel lines the desired distance apart on a piece of typing paper or thin brown paper. These will act as guidelines to keep the fabric even while the embroidery is being worked. Baste one piece of fabric along the left-hand pencil line as shown, and then baste the other piece along the other line.

③ Join the edges with fagoting, using a suitable weight of embroidery thread for the type of fabric.

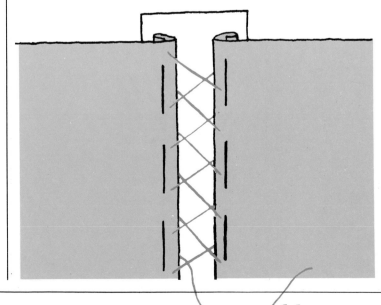

PIPED SEAMS

Piped seams are used on both garments and household accessories to accentuate the construction lines. The piping can be left unfilled to give a soft look, or filled with a length of cord – when it is known as cording – for a more pronounced line. A matching or contrasting color can be used for the piping fabric. A piped seam is quite stiff, even when left unfilled, and is unsuitable for softly draped home furnishings or garments.

PIPED SEAM

① Cut bias strips of the piping fabric approximately 1¼ inches (3cm) wide and join them together into a long strip. Alternatively, ready-made bias binding could be used.

② Fold the strip in half lengthwise with the wrong sides facing and press. Baste the folded strip along the seamline on the right side of one of the seam edges with the raw edges facing outward.

③ Place the second piece of fabric over the strip with the right sides together. Baste through all the layers, turning the fabric back occasionally to check that the seamlines match. Stitch close to the basting. Remove the basting and press. Trim away any excess piping at the ends of the seam.

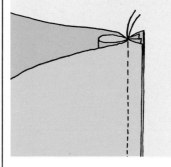

CORDED SEAM

In this type of seamline, a bias strip is folded in half around a length of cotton filler cord. This cord is available in several different thicknesses and may need to be pre-shrunk before use. The bias strip needs to be wide enough to accommodate the cord and to leave a seam allowance of ⅝ inch (1.5cm) at each side.

① Cut bias strips of the cording fabric and join them together. Wrap the strip around the cord with the right side facing outward and pin through both layers of fabric. Stitch, using a zipper foot, as close as possible to the cord. Baste the piping to the seamline and finish as for a piped seam.

② Where the cording meets around a shape, trim the ends of the cord so they butt together. Trim the fabric strip, leaving an overlap of ⅜ inch (1cm). Turn under ¼ inch (5mm) on one end, place it over the opposite raw edge and slipstitch along the joining.

SPECIAL SEAMS

Special seams are used for particular types of fabric which can be a little tricky to sew — for example, stretch fabrics and velvet.

STRETCH FABRIC SEAM

Stretch fabric must be sewn with a stitch that allows the fabric to "give," otherwise the stitching may break during use.

① Stitch as for a flat seam, using a narrow zigzag stitch, a special stretch stitch setting, or a narrow three-step zigzag stitch.

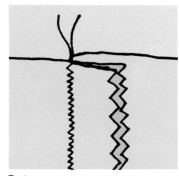

② If your machine has only a straight stitch setting, stretch the fabric gently with your hands as it passes under the needle. Use a smaller than normal stitch and polyester thread.

LACE SEAM

This seam is used on patterned lace to give an almost invisible joining. Use a thread that matches the color of lace perfectly.

① Cut out the lace with a slightly wider seam allowance than usual and mark the seamlines with tailor's tacks. Placing both pieces right side up, lap one piece over the other, taking care to match the seamlines exactly. Use a row of basting near the seamline to mark out a stitching line, following the pattern of the lace as closely as possible.

② Work over the basted line with a close zigzag stitch. Remove the basting and carefully trim away the excess lace on both the top and the bottom piece. Press the joining with the right side down on a well-padded surface.

VELVET SEAM

Use a velvet seam on any kind of pile fabric.
① Place the two pieces of fabric together with the right sides facing. Baste along the seamline following the direction of the pile. Do not fasten off the basting thread.
② Stitch the seam in the same direction, cutting the basting stitches as necessary to allow the top piece of fabric to move.

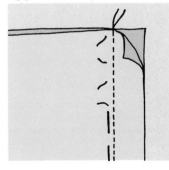

HAIRLINE SEAM

A hairline seam is used on fine fabrics where a normal seam allowance would show through and look untidy. It can also be used for a full, gathered garment where a bulky seam would be unsightly.
① Place the pieces together with right sides facing. Pin and baste just outside the seamline.

② Stitch along the seamline using a narrow, close zigzag stitch. Remove the basting and trim the seam allowance close to the stitching.

The raw edges that are left on the wrong side of those seams that are not self-finishing should be finished in order to prevent the fabric from fraying. Cutting out the pattern pieces with a pair of pinking shears will usually be sufficient to prevent most closely woven and some knitted fabrics from fraying. However, if the item is going to be washed frequently or by machine, finish the edges by one of the methods described below. Always finish the edges of fabrics that look as if they are likely to fray.

THREE-STEP ZIGZAG STITCH

This stitch is included on many modern machines. It is very stretchy, which makes it useful for finishing the edges on knits and other stretch fabrics. Work from the right side and stitch along each edge, keeping the row of stitches close to the edge, without taking the stitching over the edge. Press the seam open.

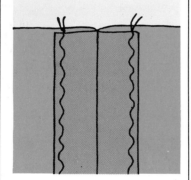

EDGE STITCHING

This is a quick and neat way of finishing the raw edges on light- and medium-weight fabrics. Fold under ⅛ inch (3mm) of the seam allowance and press the fold. Placing the right side uppermost, stitch close to the fold with a straight machine stitch and press the seam open.

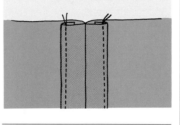

ZIGZAG STITCHING

A zigzag-edged seam is ideal for finishing the raw edges on fabrics that fray badly. Set the machine to the appropriate stitch length and width of zigzag. Stitch along the right side of the edge so that the needle stitches once into the fabric and then once over the edge. Press the seam open.

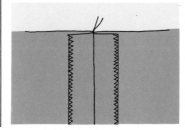

FINISHING BY HAND

Finish the raw edges by working a row of overcasting over them. Leave the stitching quite loose, for the fabric edges may curl and make a ridge if the stitching is too tight. Overcasting can be used on most types of fabric.

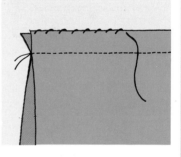

SEAM BINDING

Seam binding can be used to finish the raw edges on heavy, bulky fabrics that fray. Fold the binding in half lengthwise and enclose the raw edge in it. Pin, baste and stitch in place. Where the seams are curved, use bias binding in preference to seam binding, since it will stretch around the curve.

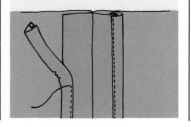

Unless a seam is a self-finishing seam, the seam allowance should be trimmed wherever the seam curves in order to leave a neat, flat seam. On heavy fabric, the seam allowance may also need to be graded to eliminate bulk.

NOTCHING

Where the seam allowance lies on the inside of a curve, cut out small "V" shapes at regular intervals almost up to the line of stitching. This is called notching and it allows the fabric to fit into the curve, giving a smooth finish.

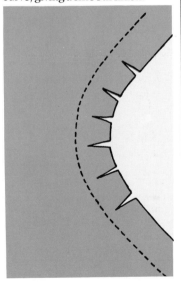

CLIPPING

Where the seam allowance lies on the outside of a curve, cut into it at frequent intervals almost up to the line of stitching. This is called clipping and it allows the fabric to spread out around the curve so that it does not pucker.

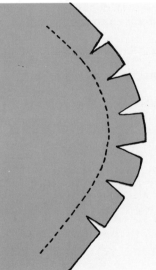

GRADING

Grading is used on seam allowances where bulk needs to be eliminated. This often happens where you have several thicknesses of fabric, such as on collars and cuffs. Trim the interfacing close to the line of stitching. Trim the under layer of fabric to within 1/8 inch (3mm) of the stitching, and then the outer layer to within 1/4 inch (5mm) of the stitching.

S H A P I N G   T E C H N I Q U E S   -   D A R T S

Fabric can be shaped in various ways, depending on the effect desired. It can be cut and joined to create a shape, controlling any extra fullness by means of pointed folds called darts. It can be gathered or folded into tucks and pleats.

The method of shaping used will influence the type of fabric required, and vice versa. A design using gathers or unpressed pleats will need a soft fabric such as silk or cotton jersey, which will drape easily. Crisp fabrics such as linen or cotton piqué can be shaped with darts, intricate seaming, and pressed pleats. Heavy fabrics including woolen tweed, wide wale corduroy and duck will have to be shaped mainly by cutting and seaming, with the addition of darts. Fabrics with bright, bold patterns need careful attention and usually work best with a simple shape, which will show the pattern to full advantage.

Another factor to consider is the extra fabric required to make pleats, tucks, and gathers. This could be important when you are intending to buy an expensive fabric such as pure silk. If you are designing an item rather than following a commercial pattern, remember to allow enough fabric for three times the width of each pleat. For gathers allow one and a half to two times as much fabric, depending on the fullness desired.

DARTS

Darts are used to provide shaping and can be curved or straight, and single- or double-pointed. The length, width, shape, and position of darts will depend on the design of the garment or item, and they may need to be altered to give a correct fit. Any corresponding darts should be realigned to match.

Darts are normally worked on the wrong side unless they are used as a decorative feature. Before stitching a dart, check the fit and adjust the position and shape of the darts as required. Darts should always taper to a fine point to fit well. Slashed darts are pressed flat and other types are pressed to one side, over a tailor's ham if necessary. Always press darts before proceeding to the next stage of assembling.

MAKING A SIMPLE DART

① Mark the position of the dart with tailor's tacks or a tracing wheel. Fold the dart in half, matching the markings carefully.

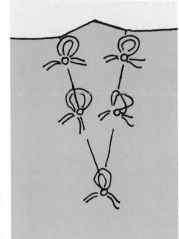

② Pin and baste the dart, starting at the raw edge and tapering it to a fine point.
③ Check the fit and adjust the dart. Remove the tailor's tacks and stitch, starting at the raw edge. Reinforce the point by working a few reverse stitches. Press as appropriate.

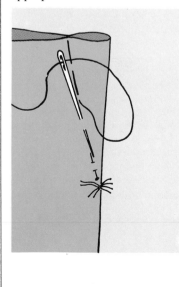

SPECIAL FINISHES FOR DARTS

Deep dart A dart which is made with a deep fold should be slashed along the fold to within ⅝ inch (1.5cm) of the point. Overcast the edges if the fabric is likely to fray, and then press the dart open.

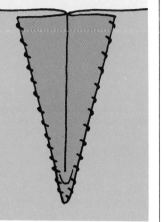

Curved dart A curved dart should be clipped along the curve, as shown. Reinforce the curve with a second line of stitching, then press to one side.

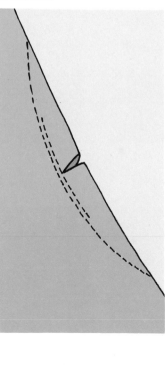

Contour dart A contour dart is pointed at both ends. After stitching the dart, clip it at the widest point almost up to the stitched line and work a second line of stitching along the curve as a reinforcement. Overcast the clipped edges if the fabric is likely to fray.

G A T H E R I N G   A N D   S H I R R I N G

Gathering and shirring are both formed by drawing up a piece of fabric by means of rows of stitching. Gathering is worked near the edge of a piece of fabric which will then be joined to an ungathered piece. Ruffles are made by this method. Shirring is worked in a band across the fabric, producing an effect similar to smocking.

GATHERING

Gathering can be worked by hand with evenly spaced rows of running stitch or on a machine using the longest stitch length available. Use a long piece of thread for the running stitch so that you can complete each section of stitching without a break.

① Work two rows of small running stitches or machine stitching ¼ inch (5mm) apart just outside the seamline. Do not fasten off the ends of the thread.

② Pull up the threads at each end of the stitching until the gathered section is the required width. Arrange the gathers evenly. Fasten the gathering threads by winding them around a pin as shown.

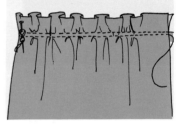

③ Pin the gathered fabric to the ungathered section, placing the right sides together and the gathered fabric on the top. The pins should be at right angles to the stitching. Baste and then stitch along the seamline. A second row of stitching should be worked to reinforce the first if the gathering is at a point of strain — for example at the waistline of a dress. Remove the pins holding the gathering threads, snip the gathering threads at the center and pull them out.

SHIRRING

Fabric can be shirred by working multiple parallel rows of straight machine stitching, using the longest stitch length.
① Draw up the threads in the same way as for gathering.

② Fold back the side edges of the fabric and stitch to secure the ends of the shirring threads.
Fabric can also be shirred on the machine using a special elastic thread called shirring elastic. This can either be threaded into the bobbin or couched directly onto the fabric with a narrow zigzag stitch.

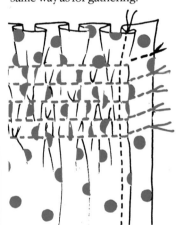

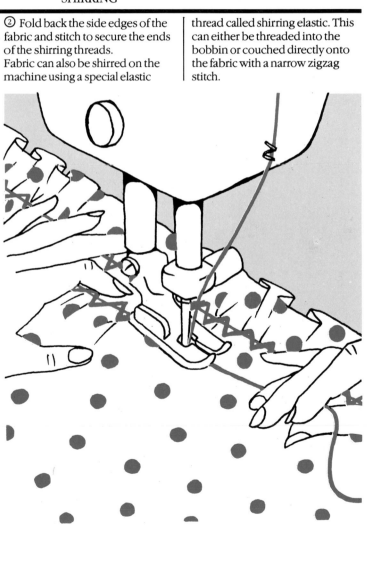

P L E A T S

Pleats are folds made in fabric and are used to distribute fullness.

There are three main types of pleat: knife pleats, box pleats and

inverted pleats. On crisp fabrics, pleats are usually pressed and can be

stitched to help them retain their shape in wear. Pleats on soft fabrics

look best when they are left unpressed. It is essential to mark the

position of pleats accurately so that each pleat takes up exactly the

same amount of fabric and the fullness is evenly distributed.

KNIFE PLEATS

The folds of knife pleats lie in the same direction along the whole pleated section.
① Mark the position of the pleats on the right side of the fabric with simplified tailor's tacks. Use a contrasting thread for the fold lines and the pleat-edge lines.

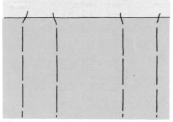

② Working from the right side, fold the pleats along the marked lines. Pin them in position with the pins at right angles to the folds. Secure the pleats with diagonal basting and remove the tailor's tacks.

BOX PLEATS

Box pleats have two folds of equal width forming each pleat. The folds turn away from each other on the right side of the fabric with the underfolds meeting at the center to form an inverted pleat on the wrong side. Box pleats are often used singly to add extra fullness, such as at the center back of a shirt.
① Mark the position of the pleats on the right side of the fabric with simplified tailor's tacks. Use a contrasting thread for the fold lines and the pleat-edge lines.

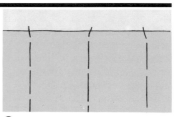

② Working from the right side, fold the pleats along the marked lines as shown, and pin them in position at right angles to the folds. Secure the pleats with diagonal basting and remove the tailor's tacks.

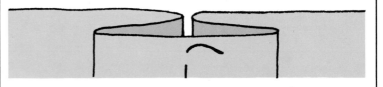

INVERTED PLEATS

Inverted pleats are the reverse of box pleats. The inverted pleats are on the right side of the fabric with box pleats formed on the wrong side. This type of pleat is often used on skirts and slipcovers.
① Mark the pleats in the same way as for box pleats. Fold pairs of pleats toward each other as shown.
② Pin the pleats in position at right angles to the folds and secure them with diagonal basting. Remove the tailor's tacks.

All pleats can be pressed, unpressed, or stitched. If the pleats are to be

pressed or stitched down to the hem, finish the hem first. When

making pressed pleats, use a damp press cloth between the iron and

the pleats to avoid making the fabric shiny. Let the fabric dry

thoroughly before removing the basting stitches. For stitched pleats,

first press the pleats in position; then stitch through the folds only

close to the edge of each pleat using a matching thread.

STITCHING KNIFE PLEATS

Stitch the edge of each pleat ⅛ inch (3mm) from the fold and finish at the appropriate point down the pleat. Pull the threads through to the wrong side and fasten off securely. Take care to make the stitched lines all the same length.

STITCHING INVERTED PLEATS

Stitch each pleat as shown, pivoting at the corners. Pull the threads through to the wrong side and fasten off securely.

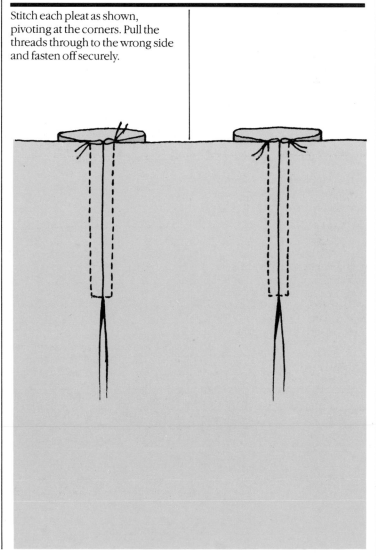

T U C K S

Tucks are really a narrow version of knife pleats held in place with stitching. They can be made in different widths; the narrowest tucks are known as pin tucks. Tucks can be placed horizontally or vertically and they are often used as a purely decorative feature on bodices and yokes. Vertical tucks can be stitched down to the hem or seamline, or the fabric can be released at a certain point to give fullness to a skirt or smock. Wide horizontal tucks are often found on children's clothes, they can be removed to lengthen a skirt or sleeves.

TUCKS

① Mark the position of the tucks with simplified tailor's tacks, using two colors of thread to denote the different lines.

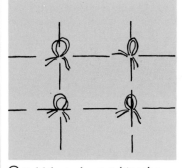

② Fold the tucks, matching the markings, and keeping the width of the tucks even. Pin and baste them in position. Stitch along each tuck and remove the basting threads. Decorative pin tucks can also be worked on fine fabrics using a twin needle, pin tuck foot and two colors of thread.

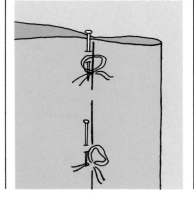

H E M S

Finishing the hem is usually the last stage in making a garment or household accessory. Hems are nearly always hand stitched to give a neat finish, but a machine stitched edge is occasionally used on a narrow hem. Use a suitable stitch and take care not to pucker the fabric by pulling the thread too tightly when stitching.

Match seam and center lines carefully and trim down the seam allowance under the hem to prevent unsightly bulges. The allowance left for a hem depends on its position and on the type of fabric being stitched. Heavy fabrics such as woolen tweed or drapery fabrics need a deep hem so that the extra weight will help the fabric to hang well. Sleeves and lightweight fabrics will require only a narrow hem. Allow bias-cut garments to hang at least overnight before marking the hem level, since the fabric may drop unevenly.

MARKING THE HEMLINE

It is best to have help marking the hemline on a skirt or dress. Use a hem marker or a yardstick and tailor's chalk to measure an even distance from the floor. If help is not at hand, pin up the hem and try on the garment in front of a full length mirror. Note any alterations, remove the garment and re-pin the hem. You may have to repeat this procedure several times before the hem is finally neat and level. Hand-operated hem markers are available which simplify this process.

To mark the hemline on draperies, hang them on the drapery rod overnight, then measure an even distance from the floor using a yardstick and chalk. Pin up the hem, then re-hang the draperies to check that the length is correct and the pattern is level.

TURNING THE HEM

Fold the hem along the chalk line and pin it up, placing the pins at right angles to the folded edge. Check that the hem is level and make any further adjustments at this stage. Baste the hem ¼ inch (5mm) above the folded edge and press it to sharpen the crease. Cut away any surplus fabric to make the hem the correct depth and trim any seam allowances inside the hem by half.

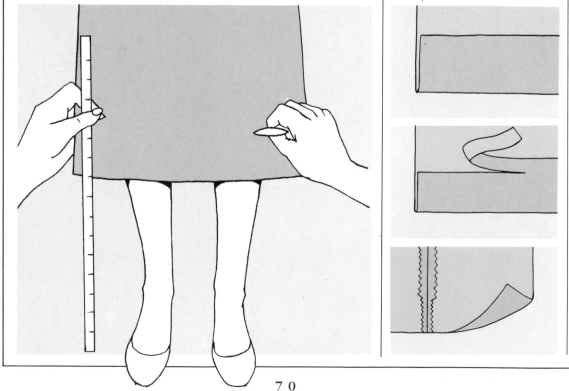

The shape of the item as well as the weight and type of fabric will determine which method of finishing to choose. Always finish hems by hand if an invisible finish is desired on the right side of the item.

PLAIN HEM

This method of finishing a hem is suitable for a straight hem on light- and medium-weight fabrics.
① Fold ¼ inch (5mm) under along the raw edge and press.
② Pin the hem edge in place, baste and finish with hemming stitch. Remove the basting and press the hem.

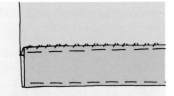

TURNED AND STITCHED HEM

A turned and stitched hem is suitable for articles that are laundered frequently and for linings. Use this method for finishing a straight hem on most weights of fabric.
① Fold under ¼ inch (5mm) along the raw edge and machine stitch near the edge of the fold.
② Press, pin, and baste the hem in place. Finish with hemming stitch. Remove the basting and press the hem.

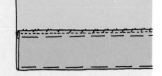

BLIND-STITCHED HEM

This finish can be used on any straight hem and is particularly suitable for use on draperies. Use either seam binding or bias binding to enclose the raw edge.
① Sew the binding ¼ inch (5mm) from the raw edge of the hem using a narrow zigzag stitch. Press the binding.
② Pin the hem edge in place, baste and finish with blind hem stitch. Remove the basting and press the hem.

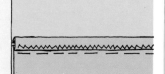

HERRINGBONE HEM

Use a herringbone hem on both loosely woven and heavyweight fabrics. The raw edge should be cut with pinking shears or enclosed with bias binding before it is stitched. This hem can also be used on stretch fabrics if your machine does not have a zigzag setting.
① Pink the raw edge or attach the binding as for a blind-stitched hem. Press, pin, and baste the hem in place.
② Stitch the hem using herringbone stitch, working from left to right. Remove the basting and press.

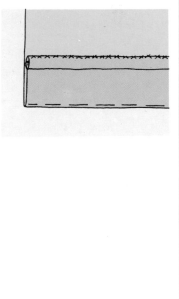

ZIGZAG HEM

A zigzag hem is used on stretch fabrics and knits. It prevents fraying and has the same amount of "give" as the fabric.

① Work a row of narrow machine zigzag or three-step zigzag stitch close to the raw edge. Press and trim close to the stitching with a pair of sharp scissors.

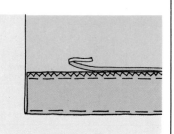

② Pin, baste, and finish with blind stitch. Remove the basting and press the hem.

EASED HEM

An eased hem is used mainly on garments to finish the hem of a flared or gored skirt. The fullness of the skirt hem is controlled by gathering the edge slightly to ease in the fullness.

① Work running stitches ¼ inch (5mm) from the raw edge. Pin up the hem, matching center and side seamlines. Draw the running stitches up to ease the fullness and fit the skirt shape.

② Shrink out the fullness using a steam iron. Remove the pins and stitch a length of bias binding to the hem, placing it over the gathering thread.

③ Pin and baste the hem in place and press, shrinking the bias binding to the curve. Finish with blind stitch. Remove the basting and press.

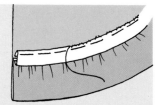

CIRCULAR HEM

A circular hem should be quite narrow so that it lies perfectly flat. Always hang a garment with a circular skirt overnight or longer before finishing the hem.

① Mark the hem line and trim away any excess fabric, leaving a hem of approximately ⅝ inch (1.5cm). Pin, baste and stitch a length of bias binding ¼ inch (5mm) from the raw edge, taking care not to stretch the binding as you stitch.

② Press the binding and then fold the fabric along the marked line. Pin, baste, and press, then finish with blind stitch or slipstitch. Remove the basting and press.

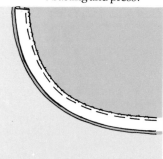

FINISHING CORNERS ON HEMS

Finish the corners on hems so they are sharp and square by mitering or facing them. Mitered corners give a good finish to tablecloths and bedspreads; faced hems are usual on garments such as coats and jackets.

MACHINE-STITCHED HEM

A narrow, machine-stitched hem is useful, since it is quick to sew and strong. The stitching is visible on the right side, so care should be taken to keep the line of stitching straight. This hem can be stitched with an ordinary presser foot as described below, or by using a narrow hemming foot.

① Trim the hem allowance to ¼ inch (5mm). Fold ⅛ inch (3mm) then another ⅛ inch (3mm) over to the wrong side and press.

② Baste along the center of the hem, then stitch close to the edge.

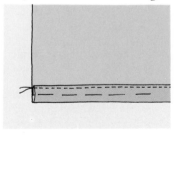

MITERED CORNERS

Hems with mitered corners can be either hand or machine stitched.

① Turn under the raw edges of the fabric and then fold the hem to the wrong side. Press it in position and open out the fabric. At the corner point of the hem fold, draw a diagonal line across the wrong side of the fabric with tailor's chalk. Cut off the corner of the fabric ¼ inch (5mm) outside this line.

② With the right sides of the fabric facing and the raw edges turned under, fold the corner. Stitch along the marked diagonal line. Turn the corner right side out, press ,and finish the hem as desired.

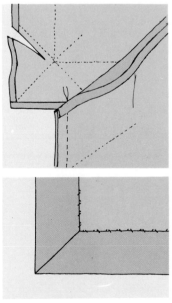

FACED CORNER

A hem with a faced corner is usually finished by hand.

① Finish the edge of the facing with zigzag stitch, or by folding ¼ inch (5mm) to the wrong side and machine stitching close to the edge. Pin, baste, and finish the hem to the desired depth.

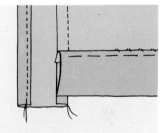

② Turn the facing back over the finished hem. Slipstitch the lower edge of facing to the hem, and then slipstitch the side of the facing to the hem to secure it.

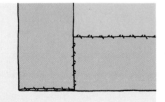

Binding is a way of finishing a raw edge by enclosing it in a strip of fabric. A contrasting color, pattern, or weight of fabric is often used, which can make it decorative.

Binding can be either single or double, except on heavy fabrics, where single binding should be used. Single binding can be bought ready for use in a variety of colors and widths; in solid-color and printed cotton, polyester cotton, mercerized cotton and a shiny rayon blend.

Binding strips can be cut from any type of fabric, although light- and medium-weight fabrics will give the best results. Leftover scraps of fabric provide a good source of binding, but if long lengths are required, buy extra fabric to avoid too many seams. The strips should be cut on the bias of the fabric, rather than along the grain, so that they will stretch easily around curves and fold over smoothly without twisting.

CUTTING THE BIAS STRIPS

For single binding, cut strips twice the required width plus a seam allowance on both sides of approximately ¼ inch (5mm). Double binding should be four times the finished width plus the two seam allowances of ¼ inch (5mm).

① Straighten the edges of the fabric by pulling the cross threads. Use the selvage as one of the straight edges if you are cutting the binding from a length of fabric.

② Lay the fabric out flat and then fold it over with a straight edge to the selvage, as shown. The diagonal fold is on the true bias of the fabric.

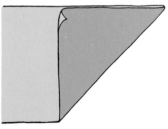

③ Pin along the diagonal, leaving the fold free, and cut along the fold. Mark a line the required distance from the fold and parallel to it. Cut along the line to give the first pair of strips. Continue marking and cutting in this way, moving the pins away from the edge each time.

JOINING THE BIAS STRIPS

Join the strips end to end, as shown, to form a strip 4 inches (10cm) longer than you need. The ends can be machine stitched ¼ inch (5mm) from the edge, or you can work a line of backstitch by hand.

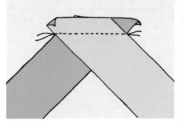

APPLYING SINGLE BINDING

① Place one edge of the bias strip right side down on the right side of the fabric to be bound, allowing ¾ inch (20mm) of binding to extend over the raw edge as shown. Take a ¼ inch (5mm) seam allowance on the binding and a normal one on the fabric. Pin across the strip at intervals and baste binding in place.

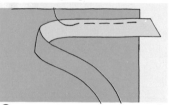

② With the bias strip on top, stitch along the seamline. Remove the basting and press the stitching. Trim the seam allowance to slightly less than the finished width of the binding. On the right side, press the binding over the raw edge.

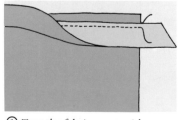

③ Turn the fabric wrong side up, fold under ¼ inch (5mm) of the binding, and bring the fold to the stitching. Baste the binding in

place in two sections, working from the center outward.
④ Hem into the line of stitching, working stitches about ¼ inch (5mm) apart. Press lightly, taking care not to flatten the binding.

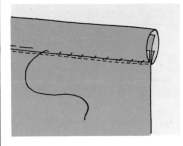

APPLYING DOUBLE BINDING

① Fold the bias strip in half with the wrong side inside and press it lightly. Baste the raw edges of the double strip to the fabric to be bound and proceed exactly as for single binding, until you reach step

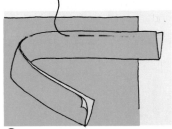

② Turn the fabric wrong side up, and roll the fold of the binding over to meet the stitched line. Baste it in place in two sections, working from the center outward. Hem into the stitching and press lightly.

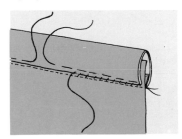

JOINING SINGLE AND DOUBLE BINDING

When binding a continuous edge such as an armhole, always make the final joining in an inconspicuous place.
① Baste the bias strip in place, leaving ⅜ inch (1cm) unstitched at the beginning and ¾ inch (2cm) overlapping at the end.

② Fold back the surplus ⅜ inch (1cm) at the beginning of the strip and lay the other end on top, as shown, to overlap the folded end.
③ Baste the ends to the fabric along the seamline. Apply the binding in the usual way.

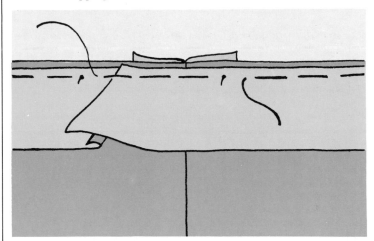

FLAT FINISH BINDING

Single binding can be applied to a raw edge in such a way that it is almost invisible from the right side, giving a neat, flat edge.
① Follow steps 1 and 2 for applying single binding.
② Turn under the ¼ inch (5mm) seam allowance and fold the binding over to the wrong side, taking it past the line of stitching, as shown.
③ Baste the edge in place and slipstitch to hold it down. Press lightly from the wrong side.

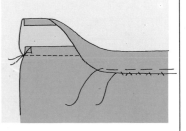

NARROW FINISH BINDING

This method of applying single binding gives a very neat finish when the main fabric is much heavier than the binding strip.
① Follow steps 1 and 2 for applying single binding.
② Trim both seam allowances down to ¹⁄₁₆ inch (2mm). Fold the free edge of the binding over to the wrong side without turning under the raw edge. Working from the right side, baste below the joining.
③ Stitch on the edge of the binding or along the seamline using a zipper foot and a straight stitch.

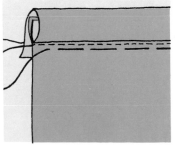

Zippers are available in three basic types: all-purpose, or conventional zippers, which have a stop at the bottom and can be used on most garments and household items; invisible zippers, which lie neatly inside a seam; and separating zippers, which are used wherever two sections of a garment must separate completely – as on a jacket, for example. Some separating zippers, called parka zippers, have a slider at each end.

All three basic types come in a variety of weights of materials. For most clothing and household accessories the usual choice is a lightweight zipper on which the teeth consist of two continuous polyester or nylon coils. When the zipper is closed, the two coils interlock. This type of zipper has the advantage of being unobtrusive and is strong enough for most purposes.

GENERAL RULES

Follow these rules when inserting a zipper to obtain a professional finish.
① Match the zipper length to the size of the opening.
② Check that the garment fits correctly before inserting the zipper.
③ Finish and press the seam before inserting the zipper.
④ Pre-shrink a zipper with cotton tape to prevent puckering if the item is to be washed rather than dry cleaned.

⑤ If the zipper is too long, shorten it at the bottom by working a few stitches over the zipper teeth 1 inch (2.5cm) below the required length and cutting off the surplus.

⑥ Pin upward from the bottom of the zipper wherever possible.
⑦ Use a zipper foot when you are machine stitching.
⑧ Finish the ends of the zipper tape after insertion.

The easiest method of inserting a conventional zipper is to place it in the center of the seam with an equal amount of fabric on each side.

③ Baste ¼ inch (5mm) from the zipper teeth and remove the pins. Stitch close to the basting on the right side using a zipper foot. Begin at the top and stitch down one side, pivot the fabric and stitch across the bottom, and up the other side. Alternatively, stitch the zipper in by hand using a tiny prick stitch and double thread. Remove the basting and finish the ends of the zipper tape.

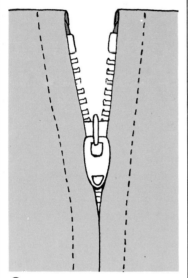

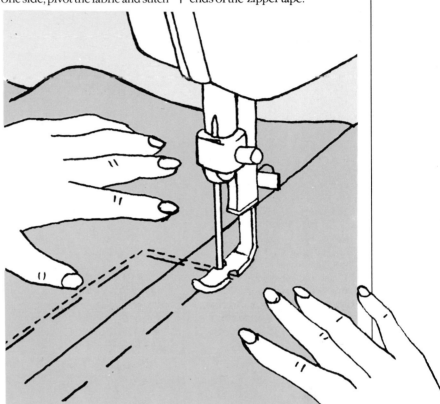

① Press the finished seam and pin and baste the seam allowances together along the fold lines. Mark the end of the opening with a pin.
② Pin the zipper in position with the teeth centered over the seam. Insert the pins at right angles to the zipper, changing the direction of every other pin.

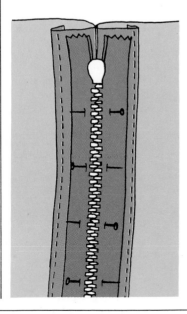

INSERTING A ZIPPER — LAPPED METHOD

In this method the zipper lies under a flap formed by the seam allowance on one side of the seam. Side zippers on garments are usually lapped so that the flap opens toward the garment back.

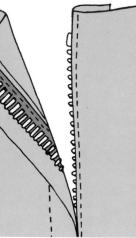

① Finish and press the seam. Working from the right side, place the zipper under the seam opening. Pin and baste one edge close to the teeth of the zipper, as shown.

② Lap the opposite seam allowance over the zipper teeth, making sure that they are completely covered. Pin and baste the flap in position $3/8$ inch (1cm) from the fold.

③ Stitch by hand or machine as for a centered zipper, step 3.

INSERTING AN INVISIBLE ZIPPER

An invisible zipper is used on tailored dresses where a conventional zipper could spoil the line of the garment. All that is visible on the right side is a plain seam and the pull tab. An invisible zipper is always stitched in place before the seam is stitched.

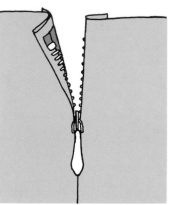

The tapes are stitched to the seam allowances of the garment pieces using a special invisible zipper foot so that none of the stitching shows on the right side. The special zipper foot must be the one recommended for the brand of zipper that is being used.

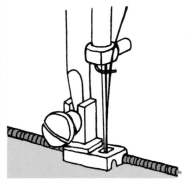

① Finish the raw edges of the fabric and mark the seamlines with basting. Open the zipper and press the tapes carefully so that the coils stand away from the tape. This will insure that the zipper will feed smoothly through the foot.

② Place the open zipper face down on the right side of one garment piece. Position one coil on the seamline with the zipper tape over the seam allowance as shown. Pin or baste in position if

necessary. Fit the right-hand groove of the special foot over the coil and stitch as far as the tab of the zipper.

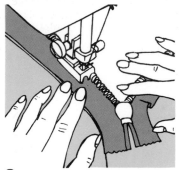

③ Pin the unstitched tape face down to the right side of the other garment piece, centering the coil on the marked seamline. Stitch in place, this time using the left-hand groove of the foot.

④ Close the zipper, then pin and baste the remainder of the seam in the usual way. Replace the special foot with an ordinary zipper foot positioned to the left of the needle. Lower the needle into the fabric slightly above and to the left of the previous stitching. Stitch the seam.

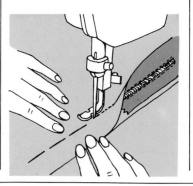

INSERTING A SEPARATING ZIPPER

A separating zipper should be inserted before any facings or hems are begun. This type of zipper is usually centered with the teeth either concealed as usual or exposed for a decorative finish.

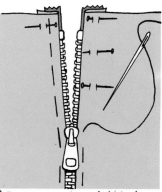

① Finish and press the raw edge. Pin and baste the seam allowances together along the fold lines.
② Pin the zipper in position with the teeth centered over the seam. Insert the pins at right angles to the zipper, changing the direction of each alternate pin.

③ Baste approximately ¼ inch (5mm) or ⅜ inch (1cm) on heavy-weight zippers, from the zipper teeth and remove the pins. Stitch close to the basting on the right side using a zipper foot. Begin at the top and stitch down one side of the zipper. Stitch the second side in the same direction. Alternatively, if you are using this type of zipper on a lightweight garment, stitch the zipper in by hand using prick stitch and double thread . Remove the basting.

FINISHING

Depending on the position of the zipper, the tape ends may be exposed, on the wrong side, after insertion. In many cases, one end of the zipper will eventually be covered by a facing, hem, or waistband and need not be finished. Exposed tape ends should be attached to the seam allowance with a row of blanket stitch. This will prevent the tape from rolling up and making a ridge.

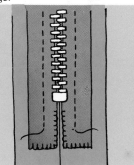

Finish the base of the zipper opening by working a small bar baste by hand on the right side. If this would spoil the look of the finished item, work the bar baste on the wrong side just below the zipper teeth.

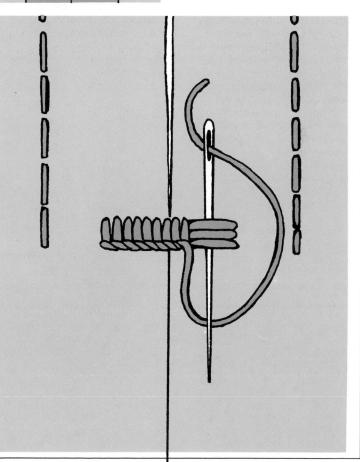

BUTTONED OPENINGS

Overlapped openings fastened by buttons are found mainly on garments. Shirts, jackets, and coats usually have a buttoned fastening on the front which can be decorative as well as functional. Small openings, especially those on children's garments, can also be fastened with buttons.

Buttonholes can be worked successfully on all fabrics provided that the right type of buttonhole is made. Button loops are much more decorative and can be substituted for buttonholes if appropriate to the style of the garment. They are also useful when a single button is necessary – for example, on a waistband. Button loops suit an edge-to-edge opening particularly well, but like buttonholes, they can also be used for an overlapped opening.

BUTTONHOLES

There are three types of buttonhole: machine-worked, hand-worked and bound. Always make the buttonholes before attaching the buttons. Horizontal buttonholes are used on the front of garments and at points of strain such as cuffs and waistbands. Vertical buttonholes should be confined to fastening loosely fitting garments and as a decorative feature, because the buttons tend to come undone if the opening is put under strain.

Calculate the size of the buttonhole by measuring the diameter of the button and then allowing a little extra for the thickness of both the button and the fabric. After calculating the size, make a trial buttonhole on a scrap of fabric in case any adjustments are needed. When marking the length of the buttonholes, use an adjustable marker set to the right measurement or a small strip of cardboard cut to size.

MACHINE-WORKED BUTTONHOLES

Machine-worked buttonholes are suitable for most types of fabric, and they are quick and easy to work. Work this type of buttonhole after all the other stages of the garment are completed.
① Mark the position and size of the buttonholes with tailor's chalk. To prevent fraying, press a rectangle of fusible web underneath each buttonhole between the garment and the facing.
② Using a zigzag foot or buttonhole attachment, stitch around the buttonhole following the instructions in your sewing machine handbook. Cut through the center of the buttonhole using sharp scissors.

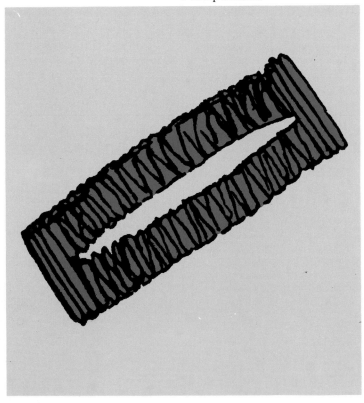

HAND-WORKED BUTTONHOLES

Hand-worked buttonholes are a little tricky, but with practice a neat finish can be obtained. If you enjoy hand sewing, you will probably choose this type of buttonhole, since it is suitable for all types of fabric. Choose a weight of thread to match the fabric and work the buttonholes after all the other stages of the garment have been completed.

① Mark the position and size of the buttonhole with lines of basting, as shown. This is preferable to marking with chalk, since the basting keeps the layers of fabric together while you are working the buttonhole. Insert a pin at each end of the buttonhole and cut a slit between the pins using a sharp pair of scissors. Remove the pins.

③ At the end of the slit, work five stitches in a semicircle to accommodate the shank of the button. These stitches should be slightly shorter than those already worked. Work along the second side of the slit in the same way as the first.

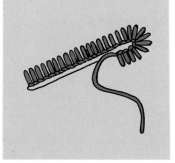

④ Work a bar of satin stitch across the end of the buttonhole to the depth of both rows of buttonhole stitch. For a more durable buttonhole, work a bar baste instead of satin stitch. Fasten off the thread on the wrong side of the garment.

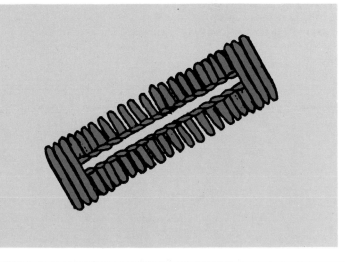

⑤ On a vertical buttonhole, work around the slit in the same way, but replace the semicircular stitches with a satin stitch bar.

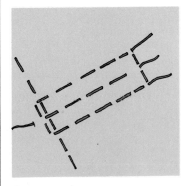

② On a horizontal buttonhole, stitch along the lower edge of the slit toward the edge of the garment using buttonhole stitch.

BOUND BUTTONHOLES

Bound buttonholes are used on light- and medium-weight fabrics. They look extremely neat and professional when worked correctly. The openings are bound with a strip of matching fabric and the first five stages should be completed after interfacing, but before the fabric facing is attached. Finish the backs of the buttonholes after the garment is completed.

① Mark the position and size of the buttonholes with lines of basting or chalk. Cut rectangles of fabric on the straight grain at least 1¼ inches (3cm) wider and longer than the buttonhole. Place the right side of the rectangle over the position mark on the right side of the garment and baste in place.

② Re-mark the buttonhole length on the rectangle. Work a rectangle of stitching around the position mark. The rectangle should be the same length as the buttonhole and three or four machine stitches wide. Work the final stitches over the first ones and cut off the thread ends. Remove the basting and press.

③ Cut a slit along the center of the stitched rectangle as shown, and clip into the corners up to the stitching.

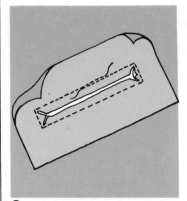

④ Push the rectangle through the slit to the wrong side. Manipulate the fabric until two folds of equal width fill the buttonhole opening, and baste the rectangle to the garment as shown. Press and then diagonally baste the folds together at the center of the buttonhole.

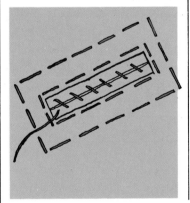

⑤ On the wrong side, the rectangle has formed an inverted pleat at each end of the opening. Hold the pleats in position with small bar tacks and remove the basting stitches. Attach the sides of the rectangle to the garment with small pieces of fusible web. Press and then finish the remaining stages of the garment.

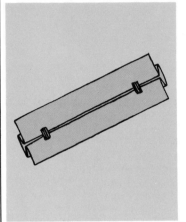

⑥ When the garment is complete, a fabric facing will cover the back of the buttonholes. Baste around the buttonholes on the right side of the garment, taking the stitches through the facing. Mark each end of the buttonhole on the wrong side by stabbing a pin through from the front.

⑦ On the wrong side, cut a slit in the facing between the pins and remove them. Turn the raw edge under with the point of a needle and hem around it to make an oval shape, as shown. Press the buttonholes on the right side and remove the basting.

Button loops are more decorative than buttonholes, and they work particularly well on edge-to-edge openings. The loops can be made singly or in strips, and they are inserted between the main piece of fabric and the facing. The loops are made from bias strips which are stitched and then turned right side out to form tubing. The loops can be self-colored or made in a contrasting color and type of fabric for extra effect.

MAKING TUBING

① Cut a bias strip of fabric the required length and about 1 inch (2.5cm) wide, joining several shorter strips if necessary. Fold the strip with the right side facing and stitch along it ⅛ to ¼ inch (3 to 5mm) from the fold. The distance from the fold depends on the weight of the fabric, so you may need to work a small sample piece first to make sure that the strip can be turned without splitting. Trim the seam allowances to minimize bulk.

② Slide a loop turner into the tube and secure the eye to the seam allowance with a few stitches. Ease the tube gently back over the eye of the turner, as shown, and pull the turner through to turn the tubing right side out.

ATTACHING BUTTON LOOPS

Measure the diameter of the button and cut the tubing into sections, allowing enough length to fit around the button plus the seam allowance at each end.

① Mark the position for the loops on the seamline on the right side of the garment. Pin the loops in place and attach them with a row of stitching just inside the seam allowance.

② Placing right sides of the fabric together, pin and baste the facing in position. Stitch along the seamline. Fold the facing back to expose the loops and press it into position. Slipstitch the facing in place.

Buttons are available in a wide selection of sizes, shapes, colors and materials. You can also buy molds made of metal or plastic to cover with fabric. Buttons should be selected carefully to make sure that they suit the weight and color of the fabric, and also the type of item to which they will be attached. When choosing buttons for a garment that has been made from a commercial pattern, be guided by the size of button suggested in the instructions, as the fastening overlap will be calculated for that size. Reinforce the fabric underneath the buttons with interfacing to prevent it from tearing or puckering in use.

POSITIONING BUTTONS

It is very important to position buttons so that they match up with the buttonholes. On an overlapping opening, pin the overlaps together first. Then pin through each buttonhole at the outer edge to mark the correct position for each button. On an edge-to-edge opening with button loops, pin the loops in position on the opposite side of the opening and then mark the placing for the buttons as above.

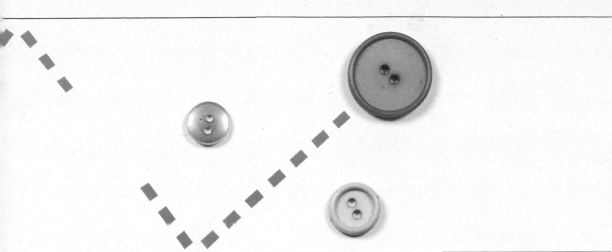

ATTACHING THE BUTTONS

Sew-through buttons are made with two or four holes right through the center, and shank buttons have a metal or plastic loop underneath the surface of the button. They are sewn on according to their construction. All buttons should be sewn on securely using a strong, matching thread. Some "give" should be left in the thread to allow the buttonhole to close under the button without distorting the fabric.

SEW-THROUGH BUTTONS

① Knot the thread and make two or three small stitches underneath the button to hide the knot. Sew in and out of the holes over a pin, as shown, leaving the thread fairly loose under the button.

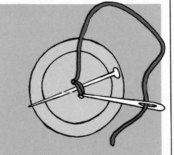

② Wind the thread around a few times between the button and the fabric to form a shank before taking it through to the wrong side. Fasten the thread securely with two or three backstitches.

SHANK BUTTONS

① Secure the thread as for a sew-through button. Hold the button at right angles to the fabric and then stitch through the loop of the button and the fabric several times.
② Take the thread through to the wrong side and fasten off securely with two or three backstitches.

O T H E R   F A S T E N E R S

HOOKS AND EYES

Hooks and eyes are useful where an extra fastening is needed on an overlap or an edge-to-edge opening — for example, at a neckline or on a waistband. Both straight and curved eyes are available; they are sewn on in basically the same way. Both types of fastening are made in black or silver-colored metal.

① Place the hook on the underside of the overlap ⅛ to ⅜ inch (3 to 10mm) in from the edge, so that the eye is concealed when fastened. Attach it to the fabric by working a close blanket stitch through the two loops at the end of the hook. Sew the neck of the hook to the fabric to keep it flat.

② Position the eye to match on the other side of the opening and attach it with a close blanket stitch worked through the two smaller loops.

SNAPS

Snaps can be used on most overlapping openings, provided there is not much strain, for they can come undone easily. They are useful for fastening items such as pillow covers, and for attaching collars that need to be washed separately from the garment. They are usually made from black- or silver-colored metal, but tiny snaps are also available in transparent plastic. The ball stud is usually placed on the right side of the underlap, with the socket on the underside of the overlap.

① Mark the position of the ball half and sew it in place by working four or more stitches into each hole.

② Mark the position of the socket by aligning the two parts of the snap and then putting a needle through the centers of both halves. Sew on the socket in the same way as for the ball half.

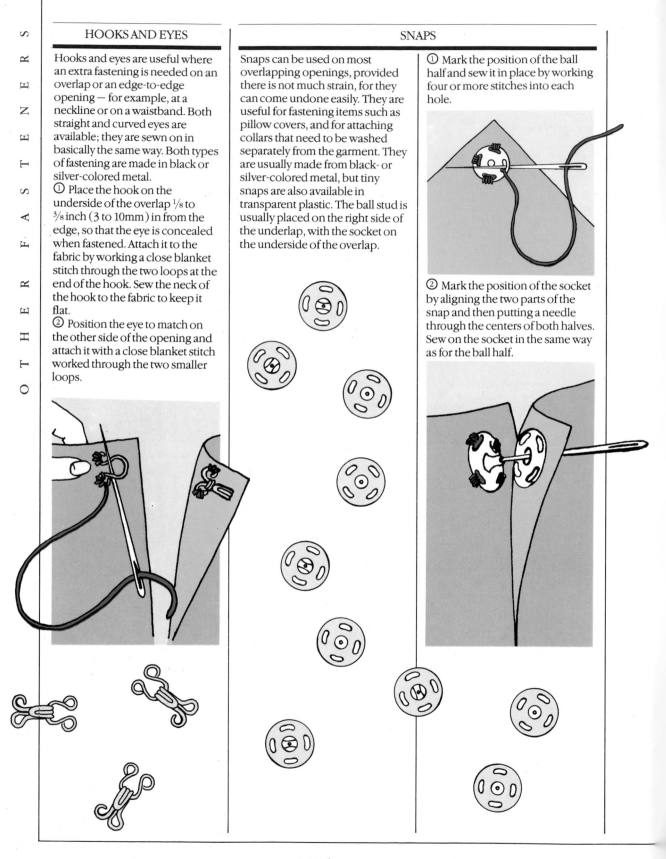

NYLON TAPE FASTENING

Nylon tape such as Velcro® is a versatile fastening strip with many applications on both garments and household accessories. It is used to fasten overlapping openings and consists of two strips, one covered with tiny hooks and the other with soft loops. When the strips are pressed together, the hooks engage in the loops.

The strips can be peeled apart quickly, so this type of fastening is useful for items such as children's garments, detachable collars, cuffs, trimmings, and pillow covers. Nylon tape fastening comes in several widths from ⅝ to 1¼ inches (1.5cm to 3cm)), and in various colors. Dots made of the same material are also available and they can be used instead .

① Cut the fastening strips to the required length and separate .
② Place one piece in position and attach by hand or machine, stitching around the edge. Repeat for the other piece.

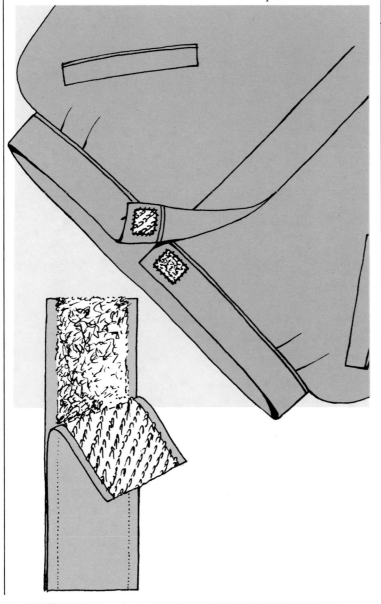

SNAP TAPE

This type of fastening consists of snaps attached at regular intervals to a length of strong cotton tape. It is used mainly on household accessories, especially comforter and pillow covers. The tape should be machine stitched to the fabric so that it is attached firmly enough. A cording or zipper foot should be used, since an ordinary foot is too wide to fit between the edge of the tape and the snaps.

① Cut the required length of tape, allowing ¾ inch (2cm) extra at each end. Make sure that the first and last snaps are an even distance from the ends of the opening.
② Pin the tape in position, turning under the extra at each end. Machine stitch along each side and across the ends.

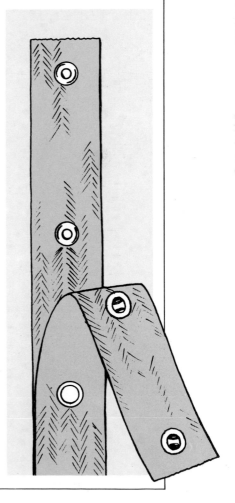

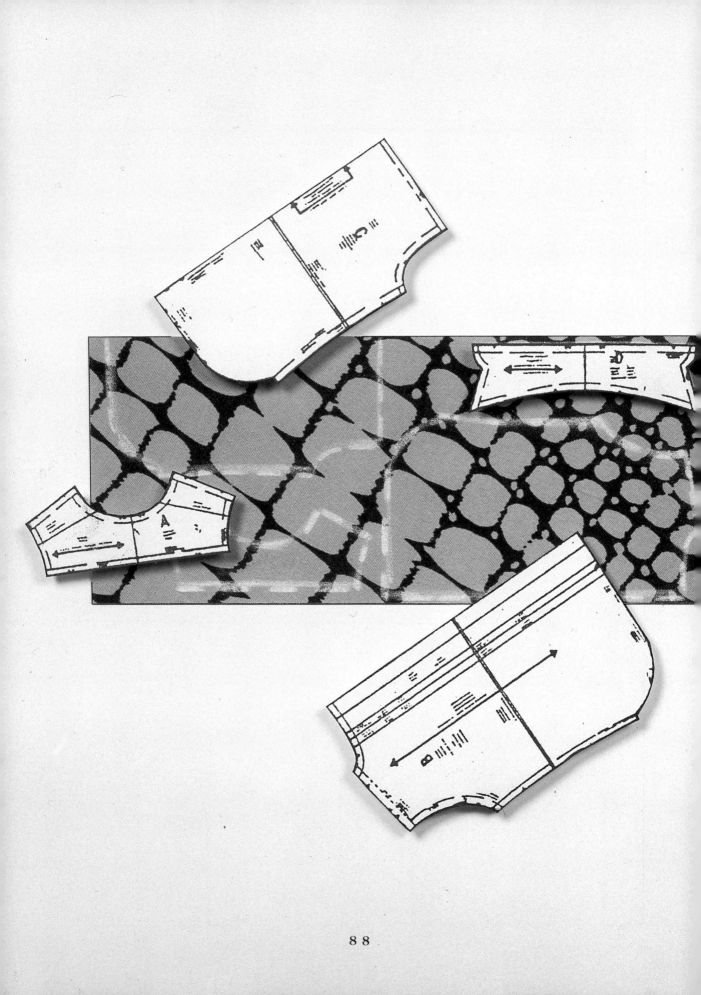

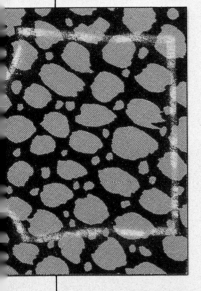

Many people prefer to make garments for both themselves and their family rather than buying them ready made. The garments are personal, less expensive, have a better fit, and there is an extensive range of fabrics and colors to choose from. This chapter takes you through the intricacies of paper patterns, and gives detailed instructions on making collars, pockets, sleeves, cuffs and waistbands.

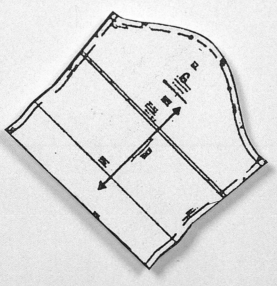

Paper patterns for garments are produced by a number of companies, and you may find that certain brands are better suited to your figure than others. You should take approximately the same size in a pattern as in a ready-made garment. If your measurements are slightly different from those on the size charts, buy a dress, blouse or jacket pattern in the size nearest to your bust measurement. It is easier to alter the waist and hips of a garment than the bust, and it is important that the pattern fit well around the shoulders and armholes. Skirt and pants patterns are bought according to hip size. Some patterns contain several sizes; these are called multi-size patterns. Most patterns offer several variations of a garment, perhaps with different sleeves, skirt lengths or collars. Each of these variations is known as a view. The fabric requirements for each view may be different.

SIZE CHARTS

① **Misses'** - to fit heights between 5ft 5in and 5ft 6in (1.65m and 1.68m) and designed for a well-proportioned figure.

② **Men's** - to fit men of average build and height about 5ft 10in (1.78m) without shoes.

①

Size	6		8		10		12		14		16	
	in	cm	in	cm	in	cm	in	cm	in	cm	in	cm
Bust	30½	78	31½	80	32½	83	34	87	36	92	38	97
Waist	23	58	24	61	25	64	26½	67	28	71	30	76
Hip	32½	83	33½	85	34½	88	36	92	38	97	40	102
Back waist length	15½	39.5	15¾	40	16	40.5	16¼	41.5	16½	42	16¾	42.5

②

Size	34		36		38		40		42		44	
	in	cm	in	cm	in	cm	in	cm	in	cm	in	cm
Chest	34	87	36	92	38	97	40	102	42	107	44	112
Waist	28	71	30	76	32	81	34	87	36	92	39	99
Hip (seat)	35	89	37	94	39	99	41	104	43	109	45	114
Neck band	14	33.5	14½	37	15	38	15½	39.5	16	40.5	16½	42
Shirt sleeve	32	81	32	81	33	84	33	84	34	87	34	87

SIZE CHARTS

③ **Half size** – to fit heights between 5ft 2in and 5ft 3in (1.57m and 1.6m) with a well-developed figure. The waist and hips are larger in proportion to the bust size in these patterns.

④ **Women's** – to fit the same height as Misses' patterns, but designed for a larger, more developed figure.

③

Size	$10\frac{1}{2}$		$12\frac{1}{2}$		$14\frac{1}{2}$		$16\frac{1}{2}$		$18\frac{1}{2}$		$20\frac{1}{2}$	
	in	cm	in	cm	in	cm	in	cm	in	cm	in	cm
Bust	33	84	35	89	37	94	39	99	41	104	43	109
Waist	27	69	29	74	31	79	33	84	35	89	$37\frac{1}{2}$	96
Hip	35	89	37	94	39	99	41	104	43	109	$45\frac{1}{2}$	116
Back waist length	15	38	$15\frac{1}{4}$	39	$15\frac{1}{2}$	39.5	$15\frac{3}{4}$	40	$15\frac{7}{8}$	40.5	16	40.5

④

Size	38		40		42		44		46		48	
	in	cm	in	cm	in	cm	in	cm	in	cm	in	cm
Bust	42	107	44	112	46	117	48	122	50	127	52	132
Waist	35	89	37	94	39	99	$41\frac{1}{2}$	105	44	112	$46\frac{1}{2}$	118
Hip	44	112	46	117	48	122	50	127	52	132	54	137
Back waist length	$17\frac{1}{4}$	44	$17\frac{3}{4}$	44	$17\frac{1}{2}$	44.5	$17\frac{3}{4}$	45	$17\frac{3}{4}$	45	$17\frac{7}{8}$	45.5

T A K I N G   M E A S U R E M E N T S

Personal measurements should be taken before you buy or alter a pattern. Get a friend to measure you if you can, since this will be easier and much more accurate. Take all the vertical measurements indicated in the diagram first, and then the horizontal ones, keeping the tape measure taut and parallel to the ground. Write down the measurements carefully and keep them safe for future reference.

BODY AND SKIRT MEASUREMENTS

- Point of bust (shoulder to bust curve)
- Chest front (armhole to armhole)
- Bust (all around body)
- Neck to waist (front)
- Waist (front)
- Waist to hem (front)
- Side waist to hem

- Shoulder to waist (front)
- Skirt yoke (front)
- Hip (front)

- Inside arm
- Shoulder
- Shoulder to waist (back)
- Nape of neck to waist (back)
- Elbow to wrist
- Back (armhole to armhole)
- Shoulder to elbow

- Waist (back)
- Upper arm
- Skirt yoke (back)
- Hip (back)

- Wrist
- Elbow
- Waist seam (back)

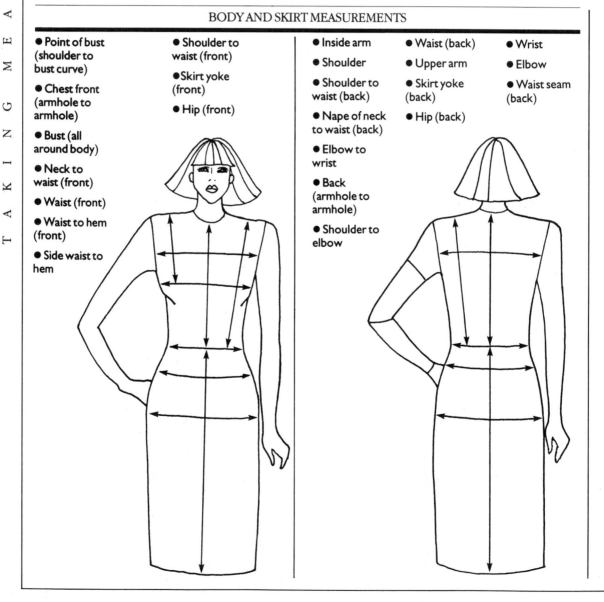

LEG MEASUREMENTS

Take waist and hip measurements (see left). Measure your inside leg from the inside top of the leg to the required height from the floor. Take your outside leg from the side waistline to the required height from the floor.

- Waist
- Hip
- Inside leg
- Outside leg

SEAT MEASUREMENTS

Sit on a chair with your back straight and measure from the side of your waist to the chair. Add ⅝in. (1.5cm) for ease but for a full figure you will need to add more.

- Waist
- Depth of crotch

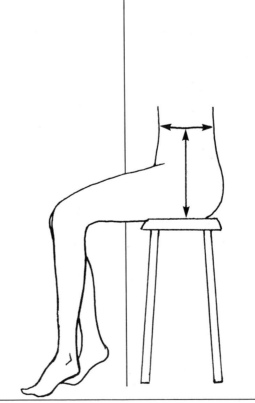

UNDERSTANDING THE PATTERN ENVELOPE

When you have bought your pattern, read the information on the back of the envelope. The most important information is in the yardage column; this tells you how much fabric to buy. Draw a ring around your size on the top row and choose the garment view and fabric width from the left-hand column. Run your finger along this line to the right until it is under your circled size. This is the amount of fabric to buy. (Metric equivalents are also included.)

There will also be a back view of the garment to show the style details, and a pattern piece

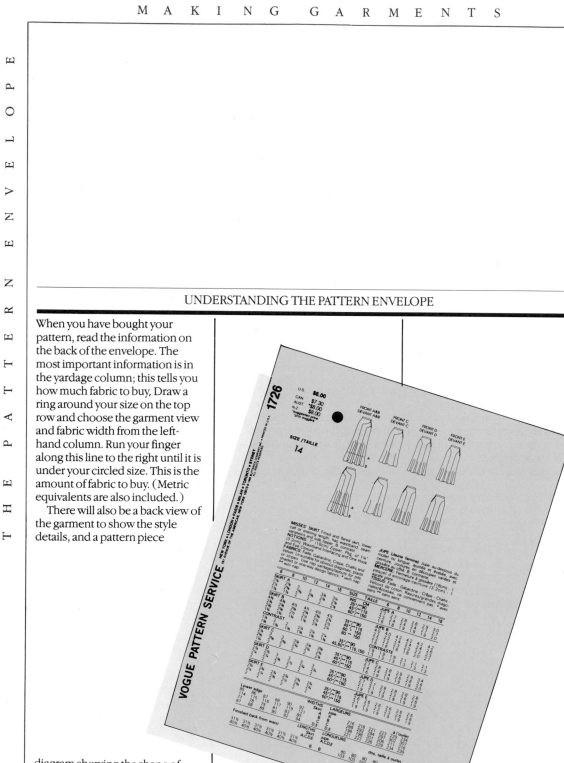

diagram showing the shape of each piece and indicating which are needed for each view. At the bottom of the envelope are the measurements of the finished garment, and a list of suitable types of fabric and sewing notions such as zippers and buttons.

ALTERING PATTERN PIECES

Spread the pattern sheets out flat and cut out all the pieces you will need for the garment. Cut exactly on the printed outlines; on a multi-size pattern follow the appropriate line for your size. Iron the pieces with a cool iron so that they are flat and easy to work with. Check all the measurements on the pattern pieces against your personal ones, measuring from inside the seam allowance if this is marked on the pattern; remember to allow for ease and style fullness. It is important to check the length of the pattern pieces, since this will make a difference to the fit of the garment. The pattern pieces will be marked with an adjustment or lengthening/shortening line. If an adjustment of more than 1 inch (2.5cm) is needed, make two smaller parallel adjustments rather than one large one.

LENGTHENING

To lengthen a pattern piece, lay it over a piece of paper and cut the pattern along the printed adjustment line. Separate the pieces until the distance between the cut edges is the same as the extra length to be inserted. Pin the pattern to the paper, keeping the cut edges of the pattern pieces parallel. Check the measurement and replace the pins with transparent tape. Trim away the excess paper carefully, following the shape of the pattern piece.

SHORTENING

To shorten a pattern piece, fold it along the adjustment line. Make a pleat to take up the length you want to remove; remember that the folded pleat is only half the width of the unfolded pleat. Pin the pleat in place and check the length. Replace the pins with tape, and trim the pattern edges so that they are even.

Other alterations to the pattern pieces are made in a similar way, by adding extra paper or by pleating the pattern to remove length or width.

Each pattern piece has a variety of symbols printed on it. Most of the marks will be transferred to the fabric before the pattern is removed and used as a guide when sewing. You should make yourself familiar with the symbols.

PATTERN SYMBOLS

Stitching line A broken line ⅝ inch (1.5cm) from the cutting line which indicates that a seam allowance of ⅝ inch (1.5cm) is included on the pattern; you will stitch along this line. If no stitching line is shown, the seam allowance may need to be added by cutting out the fabric ⅝ inch (1.5cm) larger than the pattern piece. Always check whether the seam allowance is included. Most multi-size patterns will not have seamlines although seam allowances are usually included.

Cutting line This is the continuous line on the outer edge of the pattern piece; you should follow this line accurately when cutting out the fabric. On a multi-size pattern, there will be several cutting lines with each one corresponding to a particular size.

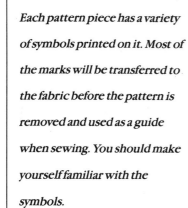

PATTERN SYMBOLS

Fold line This is represented by a line with arrows at right angles at each end, pointing to the edge of the pattern. This edge is placed on a fold of fabric so that the piece unfolds to a single whole piece after cutting out.

Grain line This is a line with arrows at each end. It should be placed parallel to the selvage so that it is on the true straight grain of the fabric.

Easing line This is represented by a short broken line with an arrow and dot at each end. It indicates a section of fabric, usually on a curve; which will need to be eased gently in order to fit the piece it is being joined to.

Dart marks The positions of the darts are indicated by broken lines which meet at a point.

Gathering line This is indicated by short broken lines with arrows at each end. Dots mark the points at each end of the rows of gathering stitches.

Buttonholes The position of the buttonholes is marked by a circle or dot with a horizontal line.

Adjustment line This is a double line, indicating where a pattern can be shortened or lengthened.

Notches These may be single, double or triple and are used to match one piece of fabric to another.

Dots, squares, and triangles These are also used for matching.

Zipper position This is indicated by a dot or notch at the base of the opening; or by a line of small triangles showing the exact position of the zipper.

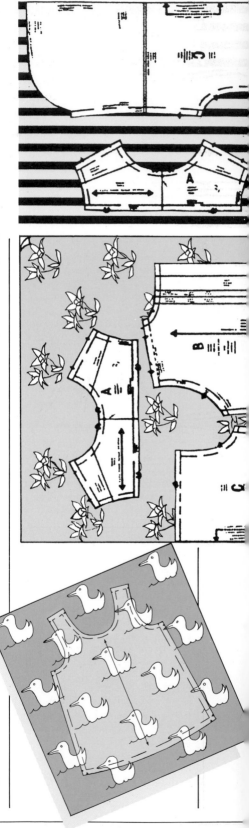

LAYING OUT THE PATTERN

(side tab, left margin)

PREPARING THE FABRIC

Plain weave fabric should have the warp and weft threads lying at right angles to each other. If they do not, the fabric is off-grain and will not hang correctly. To check the straightness of the grain, cut through the selvage at one edge of the fabric. Pull one of the weft threads which run across to the other selvage gently, gathering up the fabric, and cut along the pulled

thread as far as you can. Repeat the process until you reach the other selvage. Fold the fabric in half lengthwise and check if the cut edge is even. If the cut edge does not meet the selvage correctly, you will need to straighten the grain by pinning the cut edges and the selvages together so wrinkles form on the fabric. Press the fabric along the lengthwise grain with a steam iron, avoiding the fold, and pressing out the wrinkles. If necessary, repeat this along the crosswise grain.

Washable fabrics should be pre-washed (and pressed if necessary) before cutting out.

LAYING OUT THE PATTERN

Assemble all the equipment that you need for cutting and lay out the fabric on a clean, flat surface. A guide will be included with the pattern pieces to show you how to lay them out on different widths of fabric. These layouts will differ for fabrics with a nap or one-way design. Check that you have all the pieces you will need before you begin to lay them out. Lay out the pieces according to the layout diagram, paying particular attention to pieces such as sleeves, pockets and facings, which may need to be cut out twice. Make sure that the pieces that need to lie on a fold do so.

You will need to alter the suggested layout if the fabric you are using has a large pattern, and you should buy a little extra fabric to allow for this. Large pattern motifs should be centered on the front and back of a garment, and also on each sleeve. Always try to cut a collar so that the pattern matches from point to point.

Fabrics with a nap or one-way design should have the pattern pieces laid out in the same direction; this will require extra fabric if the pattern does not include a nap layout. The diagram shows a layout for a fabric with a one-way design.

Checks, plaids and stripes should match at the side and center seams, waistlines, armholes and sleeves. It is a good idea to choose a pattern without too

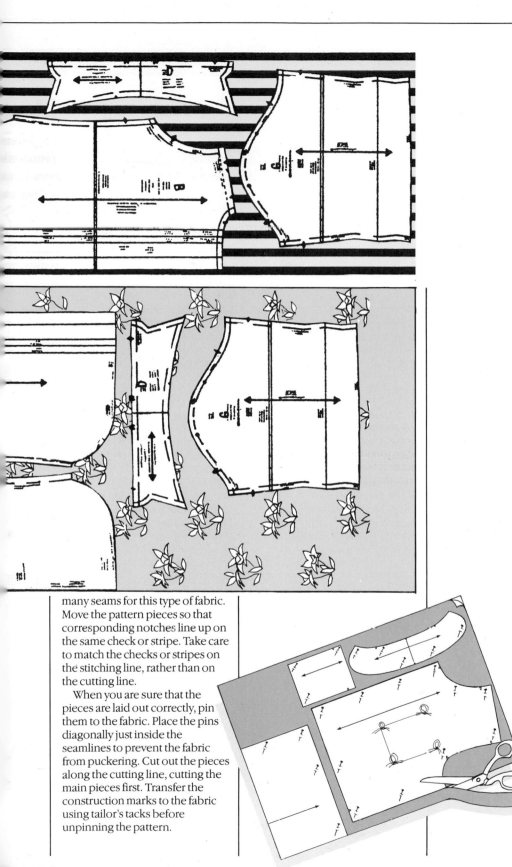

many seams for this type of fabric. Move the pattern pieces so that corresponding notches line up on the same check or stripe. Take care to match the checks or stripes on the stitching line, rather than on the cutting line.

When you are sure that the pieces are laid out correctly, pin them to the fabric. Place the pins diagonally just inside the seamlines to prevent the fabric from puckering. Cut out the pieces along the cutting line, cutting the main pieces first. Transfer the construction marks to the fabric using tailor's tacks before unpinning the pattern.

A S S E M B L I N G G A R M E N T S

ORDER OF ASSEMBLING

Assembling a garment is a fairly straightforward process if it is done in a logical sequence. For example, if you are making a dress with a waistline seam, make the bodice and skirt separately and then join them together. The instructions supplied with your pattern will tell you the correct sequence for the particular garment you are making, and they should be followed meticulously, step by step. However, there are a few rules to bear in mind.

● Each section of the garment – bodice, skirt, sleeves, cuffs, collar and pockets – should be made first and then joined to the others to form the complete garment.

● Always baste the main seams and darts by hand and make any fitting alterations before machine stitching. This will prevent your having to rip out the machine stitches, which can leave a permanent mark. Transfer any alterations to the paper pattern in case you wish to make the garment again.

● Test the stitch tension and length first on a scrap of fabric.

● Finish the seams as you go along and press each seam and dart as it is completed.

● When pressing, put the iron on the fabric along the grain, never across the grain. Do not use undue pressure or the fabric could stretch out of shape. Use a press cloth on all fabrics except cotton and linen and press on the wrong side of the fabric to prevent shine. Take great care when pressing bulky areas and do not press over pins. Press using a sleeveboard and a tailor's ham in the appropriate areas.

FITTING GARMENTS

Once the main seams and darts have been basted, pin the other seams together. Try on the garment, wearing the underwear and shoes that you intend to wear with it when it is finished. Try it on right side out and pin any openings together. Put on a belt if there is to be one, and check the fit of the garment in front of a full-length mirror.

The garment should feel comfortable when you sit down, stretch and bend. Any excess fabric will need to be taken into the appropriate seam or dart; some seams may have to be let out slightly. If any adjustments have to be made, remove the basting stitches and pin the alterations before trying on the garment again. When you are satisfied with the fit, baste the seams and begin stitching.

Follow this checklist when you try on a garment:

● The shoulder seam should be on top of the shoulder and not slope to the front or to the back. If this happens, you will have to adjust the seam slightly.

● Bust darts should point to the fullest part of the bust. Sleeve darts should point to the elbow. Adjust the darts if necessary.

● Necklines should fit snugly without gaping. A badly fitting neckline can be corrected by taking in the center back and shoulder seams or by making tiny darts at the back of the neck.

● Side, back and front seams should run in a straight, vertical line.

● The waistline seam should be in the correct position.

Interfacing is an extra layer of fabric placed between layers of the garment fabric. It adds body and permanent shape to the garment as well as reinforcing on the fabric. The type of interfacing to use will depend both on the type of garment and on the fabric from which it is made. Interfacing should never be heavier in weight than the garment fabric.

Interfacing comes in various weights and degrees of firmness; some types may be sewn in and others are ironed onto the fabric. Your paper pattern will tell you which garment pieces will need interfacing. The chart shows suitable types of interfacing for garments and fabrics.

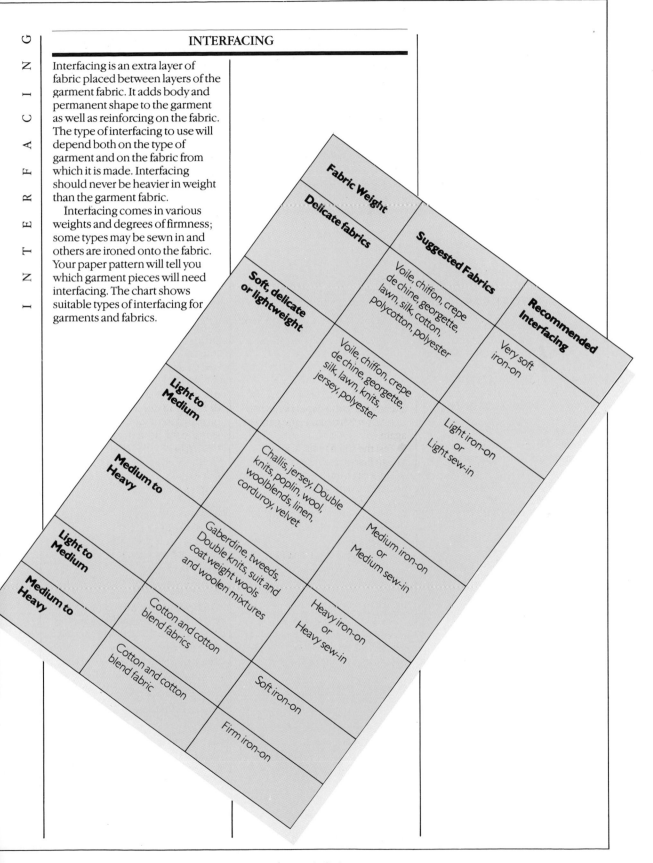

Fabric Weight	Suggested Fabrics	Recommended Interfacing
Delicate fabrics		
Soft, delicate or lightweight	Voile, chiffon, crepe de chine, georgette, lawn, silk, cotton, polycotton, polyester	Very soft iron-on
Light to Medium	Voile, chiffon, crepe de chine, georgette, silk, lawn, knits, jersey, polyester	Light iron-on or Light sew-in
Medium to Heavy	Challis, jersey, Double knits, poplin, wool, woolblends, linen, corduroy, velvet	Medium iron-on or Medium sew-in
Light to Medium	Gaberdine, tweeds, Double knits, suit and coat weight wools and woolen mixtures	Heavy iron-on or Heavy sew-in
Medium to Heavy	Cotton and cotton blend fabrics	Soft iron-on
	Cotton and cotton blend fabric	Firm iron-on

L I N I N G

Lining a garment will help to prolong its life, since it prevents the fabric from becoming baggy and pulling out of shape. Lining also finishes the inside by covering the seam edges – essential on a jacket or coat. A lining will also make an outer garment more comfortable to wear, since it will prevent the fabric from sticking to the garments underneath.

A loose lining, which is made separately from the garment and attached later, is the easiest type to make. The lining should be the same size as the garment and made without stitching details such as darts. It should fit without pulling or straining. Fabrics for lining should be slippery and quite soft. The most commonly used materials are fine synthetics and inexpensive silks.

On lined skirts and dresses, the hem of the lining is finished separately from the garment hem.

LINING

① Finish the hem of the garment in the appropriate way. Turn the garment inside out and fold back the excess lining at the hem, so that the fold of the lining hem is 1 inch (2.5cm) from the hemline of the garment. Trim away any surplus lining from the hem.

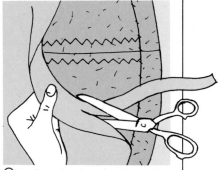

② Tuck under the raw edge and pin and baste the lining hem in place. Take care not to catch the fabric hem in the stitches. Machine stitch around the hem to provide a durable finish.

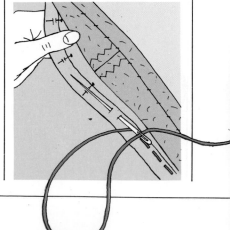

LINING

③ Secure the lining to the garment at the side seams by making three or four long stitches, as shown. Reinforce the stitches by working over them with a blanket stitch.

④ The linings of jackets and some coats are slipstitched to the finished garment hem, as shown.

Necklines are finished by adding a collar, by binding the raw edge with a bias strip or by attaching a matching piece of fabric called a facing. Armholes on sleeveless garments are also finished with a facing or a binding. The bodice darts and shoulder seams should be finished and the zipper inserted before the facing is added. Interfacing can be added to the facing pieces before stitching to give the neckline a firmer finish.

FACING A ROUND NECK

① Join the facing at the shoulder seams and finish the seams. Press the seams open. Finish the edge of the facing that will not be attached to the garment by turning ¼ inch (5mm) to the wrong side and stitching it in place.
② Pin the facing to the garment with the right sides together, matching the shoulder seams and notches. Baste and stitch it in place.
③ Trim the facing seam allowance to ⅛ inch (3mm) and the garment seam allowance to ¼ inch (5mm). Clip the curves and trim away excess fabric where the seams cross the stitched line. Press seam.

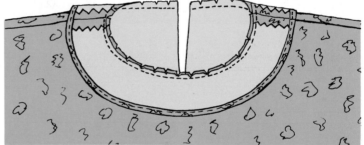

④ Pull the facing to the outside of the neckline. Stitch around the neckline through both the facing and the seam allowances. Stitch as close to the seamline as possible and press the stitching.
⑤ Turn the facing to the inside so that the seamline lies inside the neckline. Baste the facing in place and press it well.
⑥ Slipstitch the facing to the garment at the shoulder seams. Fold in the edges along the seamline at the ends of the facing and slipstitch them in place along the zipper.

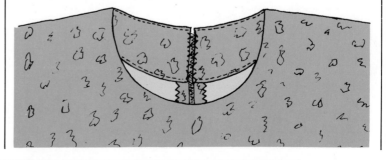

FACING A SQUARE NECK

Follow the instructions for facing a round neck, but pivot the fabric when stitching the corners, and clip the corners to within ⅛ inch (3mm) of the seamline.

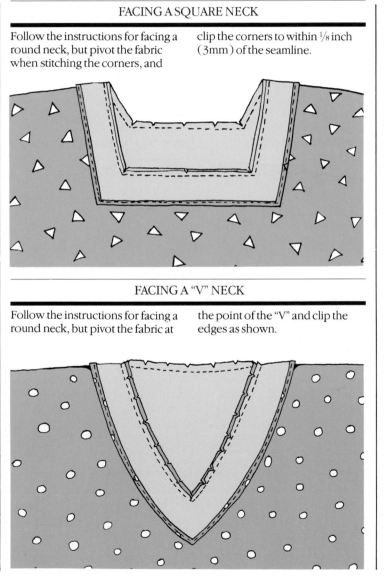

FACING A "V" NECK

Follow the instructions for facing a round neck, but pivot the fabric at the point of the "V" and clip the edges as shown.

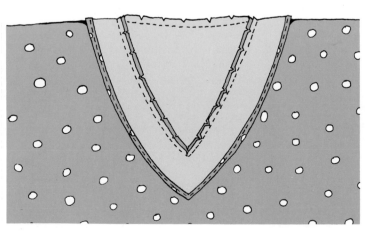

C O L L A R S

Styles of collar vary, but the methods for attaching them to a garment are virtually the same. The neckline of the garment and the neck edge of the collar must match perfectly in order to give a good fit. All matching notches should line up and the collar seam allowances should be trimmed to minimize bulk.

TWO PIECE COLLAR

MANDARIN COLLAR

ROLL COLLAR | SHIRT COLLAR WITH STAND | COLLAR WITH FACING

MAKING A TWO-PIECE COLLAR

This type of collar consists of an upper and under collar and an interfacing.

① Pin and baste the interfacing to the wrong side of the upper collar. If you are using iron-on interfacing, press it to the wrong side of the upper collar following the manufacturer's instructions.

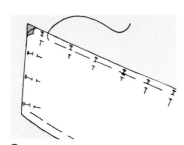

② Place the upper collar and the under collar together with the right sides facing. Pin and baste around the outer edge, leaving the neck edge open.

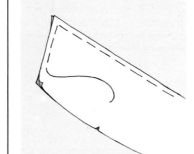

③ Stitch along the seamline around the outer edge. Trim the interfacing close to the stitched line. Trim the under collar seam allowance to ⅛ inch (3mm), and the upper collar allowance to ¼ inch (5mm). Clip any curves almost to the line of stitching.

④ Press the stitching. On a round collar, turn the collar to the right side and baste near the edge to hold the layers in place. Press.

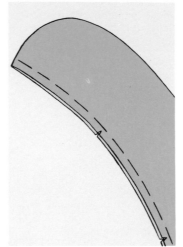

⑤ On a pointed collar, strengthen the corners with a few smaller stitches and trim the seam allowances across the points. Turn it right side out and gently push the points out with a bodkin or fine knitting needle. Baste and press as above.

⑥ Attach a two-piece collar by the second method described.

MAKING A MANDARIN COLLAR

This type of collar is close fitting and stands up around the neckline. It can have an opening at the front or at the back. It is cut on the bias and must be interfaced.

① Apply the interfacing to the wrong side of the outer collar. Pin the outer and inner collars together with the right sides facing and baste together, leaving the neck edge open.

② Stick along the seamline. Trim the interfacing close to the stitched line and the seam allowances down to ¼ inch (5mm). Cut across the corners close to the stitched line, and clip the curved edge.

③ Turn the collar right side out. Pin and baste along the edge and press well. Attach the collar to the garment using the second method described.

MAKING A ROLL COLLAR

A roll collar is made from one piece of fabric cut on the bias and folded in half before stitching. It is folded again when it is worn to give a soft neckline. This type of collar does not need interfacing and it can be attached by either of the methods described.

① Fold the collar in half with the right sides facing and notches matching. Baste along each end.

② Stitch the ends, leaving the neck edge open. Trim the seam allowance of the inner half of the collar to ⅛ inch (3mm) and that of the outer to ¼ inch (5mm). Cut across the corners.

③ Turn the collar right side out and push out the corners gently. Press seams, avoiding the fold.

MAKING A SHIRT COLLAR WITH A STAND

This collar consists of a two-piece collar which is mounted on a stand to give it height.
① Make the two-piece collar as described above. Interface the wrong side of the outer stand.
② Insert the assembled collar between the two pieces of the stand with right sides facing and notches matching. Pin and baste through all the layers and then stitch along the seamline.

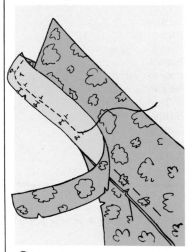

③ Trim the interfacings and the seam allowances and grade them to eliminate bulk.
④ Turn the stand right side out and press it. Attach it to the garment by the first method described.

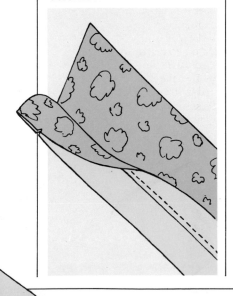

ATTACHING A COLLAR WITHOUT A FACING

If the garment has an opening, it should be finished before the collar is attached.
① Place the under collar on the neckline of the garment with right sides together and notches matching. Pin the under collar to the garment.

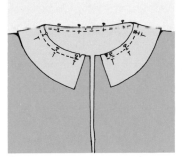

② Stitch along the seamline and trim the seam allowances to ¼ inch (5mm). Fold the collar up and tuck the trimmed seam allowance into the collar. Press it in place.

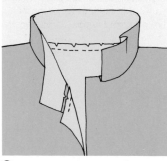

③ Turn under the seam allowance on the upper collar. Pin and baste it in position as shown. Slipstitch it to the garment along the seamline.

ATTACHING A COLLAR WITH A FACING

If a collar is made in two pieces without a stand this method of attachment is best.
① Place the collar on the garment neckline with the under collar to the right side of the garment. Lay the facing over it with the right sides facing and notches matching.
② Pin the layers together and baste in place. Stitch along the seamline of the facing. Trim the seam allowances and corners and clip the curve of the neckline almost up to the stitched line.

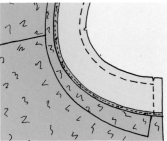

③ Fold the facing to the inside of the garment and push out the corners. Baste the facing in place and press it well.

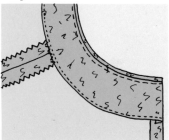

④ Slipstitch the facing to the garment where it crosses the seams.

There are several different styles of sleeve but they are all based on one of the following three types.

SET-IN SLEEVE

This is the most common type of sleeve. It is cut separately from the garment and inserted into the armhole. The length and width of the sleeve can differ, but the method of insertion is the same. Finish seams and the lower edge of the sleeve as desired before inserting it.

① Stitch two rows of gathering between the notches at sleeve cap. Turn the sleeve right side out and position it in the armhole, with the right sides of the fabric facing.

② Pin at the underarm, shoulder seam and notches, working from the inside of the sleeve and setting the pins at right angles to the edge of the fabric. Gather up the fullness at both sides of the sleeve toward the shoulder line until it fits the armhole exactly.

③ Spread the gathers evenly and pin this section of the sleeve to the armhole. Baste and stitch the sleeve in place, starting at the underarm seam.

④ Remove the gathering stitches and trim the seam allowances slightly. Finish the raw edges and press the seam.

RAGLAN SLEEVE

A raglan sleeve is attached to the back and front of the garment with a long diagonal seam running underneath the arm.

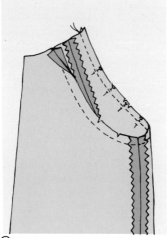

① Pin, baste, and stitch the shoulder dart if the sleeve is cut in one piece. Slash the dart and finish the edges as appropriate. For a two-piece sleeve, pin, baste, and stitch the shoulder seam and finish the edges.

② Pin, baste, and stitch the underarm seam of the sleeve and the side seam of the garment. Finish the edges and press the seams open.

③ Turn the sleeve right side out and pin it to the garment with the right sides facing and notches matching. Baste and stitch in a continuous line from one neck edge to the other. Remove the basting stitches.

④ Clip and notch the seams along the curves so that they will lie flat. Finish the edges and press the seams to one side.

KIMONO SLEEVE

Kimono sleeves are usually cut in one piece with the body of the garment.

① Placing right sides together, pin, baste, and stitch the side and underarm seams. Shorten the stitch length on the curve to make the seam stronger.

② Clip the curves at intervals and finish the raw edges. Press the seams open. Baste a 6 inch (15cm) length of straight seam binding along the curve of the underarm seam on the wrong side.

③ On the right side of the garment, stitch two parallel lines each 1/8 inch (3mm) from the seamline. Pull the thread ends through to the wrong side and tie them securely.

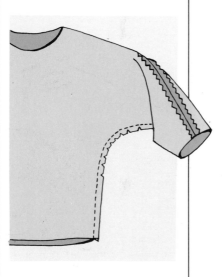

If you intend to add a cuff, you will have to make an opening in the sleeve to allow your hand to go through easily. The opening should be finished before the cuff is attached. Sleeve openings are placed on the side of the sleeve toward the back. They can be finished with either a facing or a narrow binding.

FACED OPENING

① Cut a strip of the garment fabric 1¼ inches (3cm) longer than the opening and 2¾ inches (7cm) wide. Finish the two long sides and one short one by turning ¼ inch (5mm) of the fabric to the wrong side and stitching in place. Placing right sides together, baste the strip over the opening with the center of the strip over the cutting line on the sleeve.

② Stitch around the opening ¼ inch (5mm) from the cutting line as shown, curving the stitching at the top of the opening. Cut to the top of the stitching.

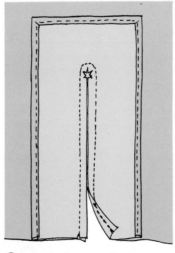

③ Turn the facing to the wrong side of the sleeve and baste it in place. Press the opening and slipstitch the facing to the sleeve. Do not remove the basting stitches until the cuff has been attached.

BOUND OPENING

① Cut the opening to within ¼ inch (5mm) of the top. Cut a bias strip of fabric twice as long as the opening plus ¾ inch (2cm). The strip should be about 1⅜ inches (3.5cm) wide.

② Placing right sides together, position one edge of the strip along the left-hand edge of the opening. Stitch along this side and then curve the strip at the top of the opening and stitch around the curve. Continue stitching along the right-hand side.

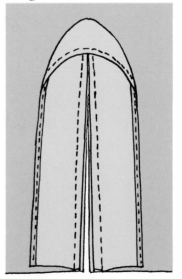

③ Reinforce the curve with a short row of smaller stitches and then finish the binding in the usual way.

The lower edge of the sleeve can be finished in various ways. A simple hem is neat on a short or three-quarter length sleeve; fuller sleeves can be finished with a cuff.

MAKING A WRAP-OVER CUFF

This cuff is used on dresses, blouses, and shirts and is cut from a straight piece of fabric. It wraps over at the opening and is fastened with buttons.

① Apply the interfacing to the wrong side of the cuff. Fold the cuff in half lengthwise with the right sides facing. Baste the ends and stitch along the seamline.

② Trim the interfacing close to the stitching. Trim the seam allowance on the inner half of the cuff to ⅛ inch (3mm) and that on the outer half of the cuff to ¼ inch (5mm). Cut the corners close to the stitching.

③ Press and turn the cuff right side out. Push out the corners so that they are sharp and press again.

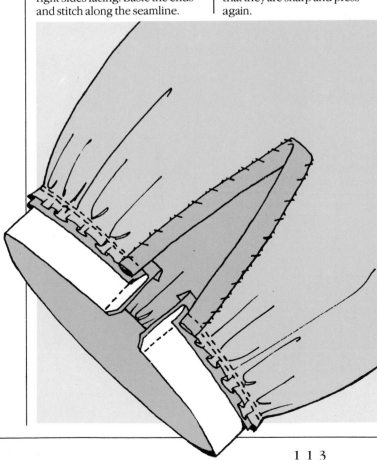

ATTACHING A BASIC CUFF

Finish the sleeve seam, check the length of the sleeve and finish the opening before attaching the cuff.

① Stitch two rows of gathering around the bottom of the sleeve. Pull up the stitches until the sleeve fits the cuff.

② Placing the right sides together, pin the interfaced half of the cuff to the sleeve, working from the sleeve side.

③ Match the notches and arrange the gathers evenly. Baste and stitch the cuff to the sleeve. Trim the seam allowances to ¼ inch (5mm).

④ Turn the cuff away from the sleeve and press the seam toward the cuff. Fold the free edge of the cuff along the seamline and slipstitch it to the machine-stitched line. Press the cuff and remove the basting stitches.

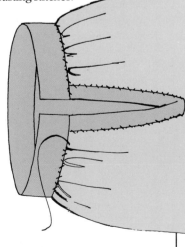

P O C K E T S

Pockets can be functional or purely decorative. They should always be firmly attached to the garment. Pockets can be made separately and added to the garment, or they can be concealed in the garment seam.

PATCH POCKET

A patch pocket is stitched onto a garment; it can have rounded or square corners at the base.

① Apply soft interfacing to the wrong side of the outer pocket. Fold the pocket in half with the right sides together and pin. Baste and stitch along the seamline, leaving an opening in the center of the lower edge for turning the pocket out.

② Trim the interfacing and seam allowances as for a collar, and cut off the corners, or notch the curves. Turn the pocket right side

out and push out corners. Slip–stitch across the opening to close it.

③ Pin and baste the pocket in position on the garment. Stitch around three sides, finishing off securely at the top corners.

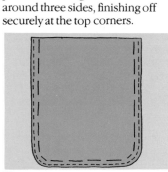

④ A flap for the pocket can be made in the same way. It should be slightly wider than the pocket, but shallower. Follow steps 1 and 2 above, and work any decorative stitching or buttonholes before attaching the flap.

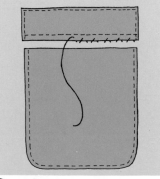

⑤ Attach the flap to the garment just above the pocket and press it downward.

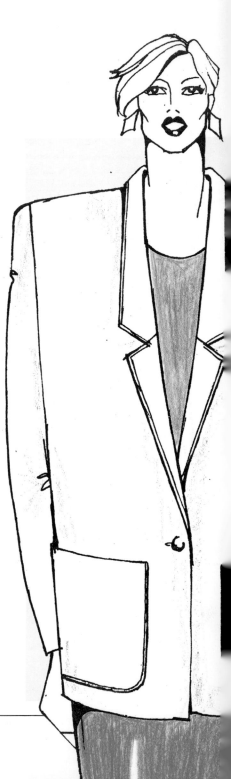

CONCEALED POCKET

A concealed pocket lies neatly in the side seam of a garment and is usually made from matching fabric.

① Place one section of the pocket, right sides facing, along the seamline of the garment between the position marks. Pin and baste in place. Stitch ⅜ inch (1 cm) from the edge between the marks and press the pocket piece away from the garment.

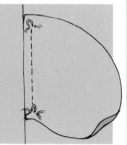

② Repeat step 1 for the other half of the pocket. With the right sides facing and notches matching, place the two garment pieces together. Pin, baste, and stitch along the seamline, pivoting the fabric at the corners to stitch the main seam and pocket seam in one operation.

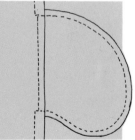

③ Press the seam, clip into the angle of the seam allowance on the back of the garment and finish the raw edges. Press the garment seam open.

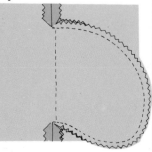

The best finish for the waistline of a skirt or pair of pants is a waistband. It should fit snugly and be firm enough not to crease during wear. An alternative finish to a stiffened band is an elasticized one, which can also be used to finish a sleeve, provided it is not too full. Waistbands are attached after the main part of the garment is finished, but before the hem is turned up.

ELASTICIZED BAND

This type of waistband is comfortable to wear and is useful for gathered skirts and pants, and for children's clothes.

① Pin a length of elastic around your waist and adjust it so that it fits comfortably. Add an extra 1 inch (2.5cm) for the overlap. The casing to take the elastic should be twice the width of the elastic plus ⅛ inch (3mm) for ease. Make the casing the length of the edge it will be joined to and allow a ⅝ inch (1.5cm) seam allowance all round.

② Stitch the ends of the casing together and press the seams open. With the right sides facing, pin, baste, and stitch one edge to the garment. Press and trim the seam allowance on the garment to ⅛ inch (3mm) and that of the casing to ¼ inch (5mm).

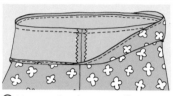

③ Turn under the seam allowance on the other edge of the casing and fold it over even with the previous stitching. Pin and baste in place. Slipstitch or machine-stitch around the casing leaving a gap of 1¼ inches (3cm) at the casing seam.

④ Attach the elastic to a bodkin or elastic threader and guide it through the casing. Pin the free end of the elastic to the garment to prevent it from disappearing into the casing. Ease the elastic through until it appears at the other side and the two ends overlap.

⑤ Unpin the ends of the elastic and overlap them by 1 inch (2.5cm). Overcast the edges together firmly. Pull the casing over the elastic and slipstitch it neatly in place along the opening.

STIFFENED BAND

Buy special waistbanding for this type of waistband, since interfacing is not quite stiff enough.

① Place the waistband on the garment waist with the right sides facing, and notches matching. Pin, baste, and stitch in place.

② Pin the strip of waistbanding to the band as shown, with the edge on the line of stitching. Baste it in place and stitch from the other side, close to the edge. Trim the garment seam allowance close to the stitching and the waistband allowance $1/8$ inch (3mm) wider.

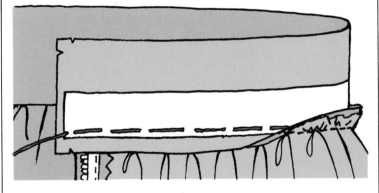

③ Fold the waistband back along the waistbanding and press the seams and the band away from the skirt. Stitch the ends of the band and trim away the surplus fabric.

④ Turn the waistband right side out and turn under the seam allowance on the unstitched edge. Pin it in place and slipstitch it to the garment.

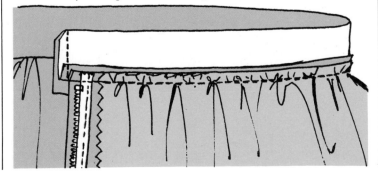

BELT CARRIERS

If you intend to wear a belt over a stiffened waistband, keep it in place by adding belt carriers. They can be stitched or made from strips of matching fabric.

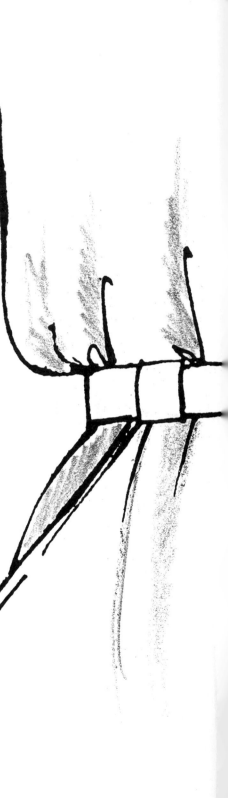

STITCHED CARRIERS

These are less prominent than fabric carriers, but not as strong. Make them from matching buttonhole twist.

① Work a double loop of thread in the right position for the belt, making it wide enough to accommodate it comfortably.

② Reinforce the loop by working blanket stitches along it, packing them tightly together.

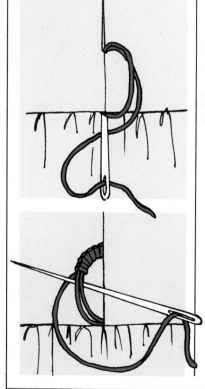

FABRIC CARRIERS

Fabric carriers are strong and should be used for a wide belt and on trousers in preference to the stitched type.

① For each carrier cut a strip of matching fabric 1¼ inches (3cm) wide and long enough to take the belt, plus 1¼ inches (3cm) for ease and seams. Fold the strip lengthwise with the right sides together.

② Pin and stitch the strip ¼ inch (5mm) from the raw edge. Trim the seam allowance to ⅛ inch (3mm) turn right side out and press with the seam the center of one side.

③ To attach each carrier, turn ¼ inch (5mm) of the fabric under at each end, then stitch it in position with the seam concealed under the carrier.

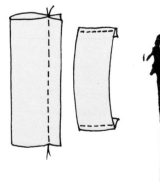

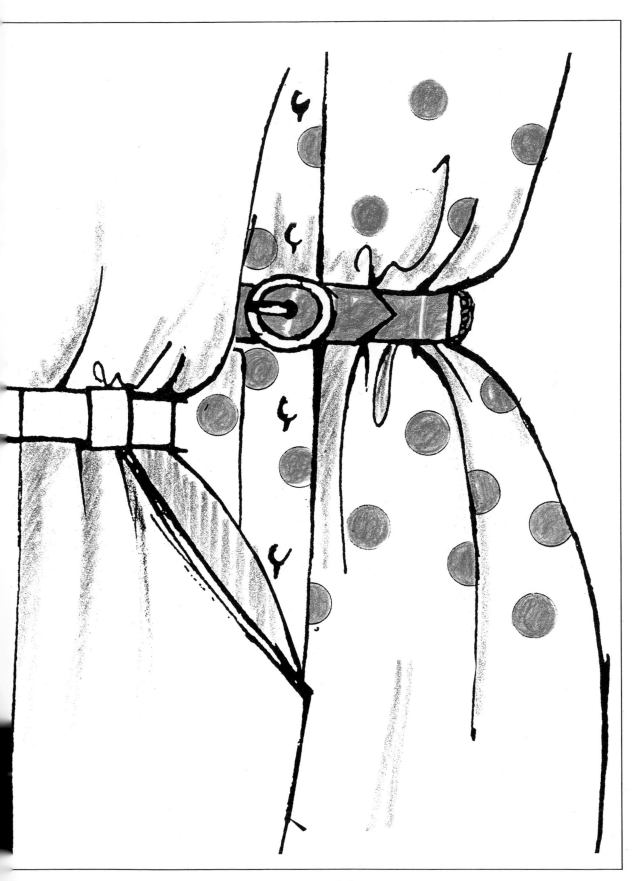

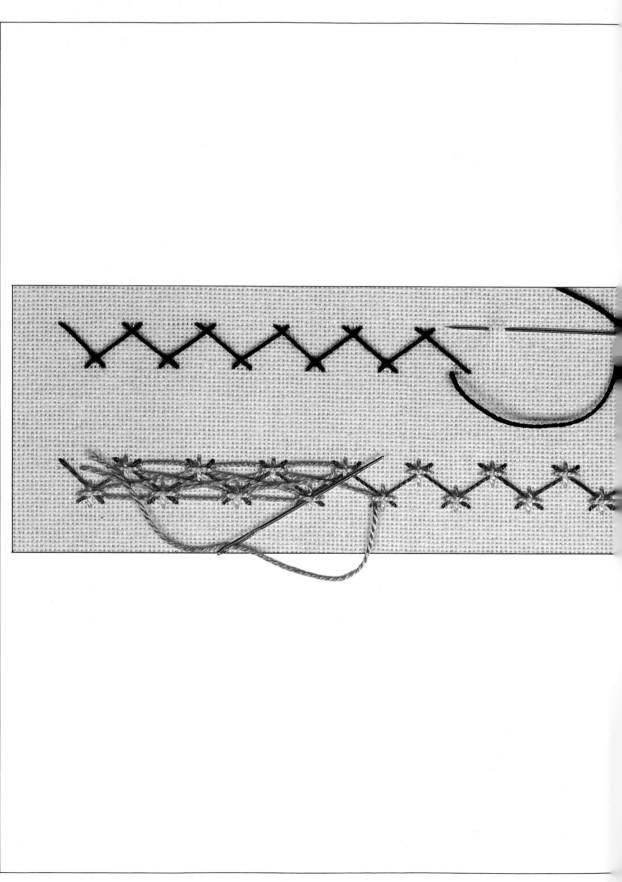

You can add a distinctive touch to your

clothing and home furnishings in many

different ways. Color is important, as is the

use of pattern and decoration. Style is very

individual and something which pleases you

visually may not please others! Probably

the best way to begin developing your own

style is to build on a simple, fairly neutral

color scheme. Gradually add touches of

different colors to react with this.

COLOR AND PATTERN

There are no hard and fast rules when choosing which particular colors to put together, for they tend to interact in different ways. You may like certain combinations and hate others: you may decide to use only dark and light tones of one color. A tonal color scheme will give a natural continuity to an outfit or a room. Another idea is to add touches of the bright primary colors, red, blue, and yellow, to a white, gray or cream basic scheme. Dark colors such as black, dark gray, and navy blue can be terrific for a basic wardrobe when accessorized with hot fuchsia pink, scarlet, or an acid yellow.

Reds, yellows, and oranges are warm to live with, while blues and greens give the impression of being cool. Pinks and mauves can be cool or warm in appearance, depending on whether the shades tend toward blue or toward red. This could be an important consideration when choosing colors for draperies and bed-linen. For example, if you have a north-facing bedroom, it will appear colder if you use shades of blue. The same room will have a sunnier aspect if you choose a warm shade of yellow for the décor instead. Light tones of a cool color will make a room look larger than it is, and dark tones will make it look smaller.

PATTERN

Fabric can be solid-color, textured or patterned. Patterns range from tiny checks, stripes, and neat, geometric designs to huge, splashy florals and abstracts. Areas of pattern on draperies or upholstery can liven up a plain expanse of a neutral color quite dramatically. A small, regular geometric print will provide a good foil for a stunning floral pattern, while two or three large patterns used together might cancel each other out visually. The same pattern can look very different when printed in other colors. A pattern in bright, garish colors may look as though it would be difficult to live with, but the same pattern could be pleasing printed in soft landscape shades of muted greens and browns.

A large pattern on clothing tends to make the wearer look bigger than would a small regular one. The same is true of light colors, shiny or heavily textured fabrics, and strong horizontal stripes.

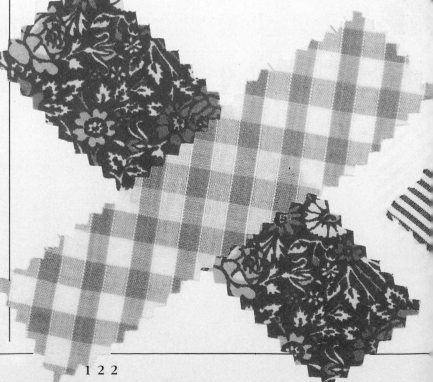

DECORATION

Fabric can be decorated simply and quickly by the addition of lace, braid, ribbon or fringe. Lace edging and fringe are usually inserted into a seam in the same way as is cording, whereas ribbon and braid are stitched directly to the fabric. Wide borders can be built up using multiple straight rows of ribbon, braid or machine embroidery, especially if you have a sewing machine that produces decorative patterns. These can be used to enhance simple garmets, table linen and pillow covers. Ornamental patterns can also be worked using ribbon and braid.

Other forms of decoration include hand embroidery, appliqué, applying beads and sequins, and quilting. Fabric can be its own decoration if it is pieced together as patchwork.

RIBBON AND BRAID

Ribbons and braids have been used for centuries to decorate clothes and accessories. When working patterns make sure that neither the background fabric nor the braid puckers, and that curves and corners are neat and well finished.

① Mark the pattern on to the background fabric with tailor's chalk or a special marking pen that will wash out. Lay the braid or ribbon on top, turning under the raw edges at the ends, and baste in place.

② Corners and angles are formed by turning the braid over as shown. When working curves, baste the outer edges of each curve in place first. Gather the inner edges of the curves until they fit the marked pattern lines and then baste them in place.

③ Stitch the braid or ribbon to the fabric along each edge using backstitch or running stitch and a matching color thread.

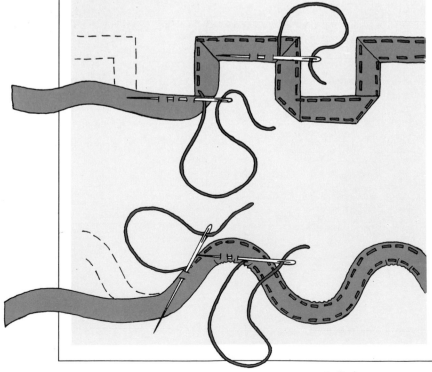

BEADS AND SEQUINS

Beads and sequins can glamorize an ordinary garment very successfully. They can be used to create single motifs or borders, and, although sewing them on by hand is quite a time-consuming process, the end result will be worthwhile.

Sequins can be applied so the stitches show on the surface or so they are concealed. If the stitches are going to show, use a pretty thread such as a twisted silk or three strands of stranded floss.

Beads can be applied individually or couched down in a continuous line. The stitches should not show on the right side of the fabric. Some beads have only a very tiny hole, so you may need to buy special beading needles for sewing them on. Use a fine, strong thread and take care to secure the beginning and end of the thread firmly.

APPLYING SEQUINS

① To apply sequins with the stitches showing, bring the needle through to the right side of the fabric and thread it through the eye of the first sequin. Work a backstitch over the right side of the sequin and bring the needle back through the fabric at the left of the sequin, ready to thread through the next one. Continue until all the sequins are sewn onto the fabric, then secure the end of the thread on the wrong side.

② To apply sequins with invisible stitches, work a backstitch over the left side of the first sequin. Place the next sequin so that it overlaps the first one and bring the needle through the fabric at the left-hand edge of the sequin. Work a backstitch from the edge of the sequin, taking the needle through the eye and inserting it into the hole of the preceding backstitch. Repeat this sequence until all the sequins are in place and secure the thread on the wrong side.

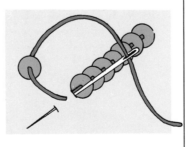

APPLYING BEADS

① To sew on beads individually, bring the needle through the fabric and thread the bead onto it. Insert the needle into the fabric through the same hole and bring it back through the fabric where you want the next bead to be placed.

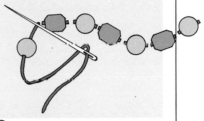

② To sew beads in a continuous line, cut two lengths of thread. Bring one thread through to the right side of the fabric and thread the beads on to it. Slide the first bead into position and, using the second thread, work a small stitch close to the bead and over the first thread, as shown. Slide the next bead into position and repeat the process. Continue in this way until all the beads have been couched onto the fabric.

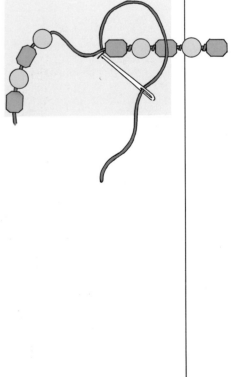

Hand embroidery has been used for centuries to embellish garments and accessories. It can be as simple or ornate as you like. Add embroidered motifs and monograms to your clothes, and borders to table linen; work larger pieces to make into stunning pillow covers. If you are new to embroidery, practice the stitches first on scraps of fabric until you feel confident using them. As with most skills, practice makes perfect, so do not be discouraged by your first attempts if they do not seem very professional.

Details are given in this section of the threads and needles used for embroidery, and instructions are provided for transferring a design to your fabric. A selection of stitches is shown in easy-to-work steps.

EMBROIDERY HOOP

All embroidery will be more successful if the fabric is held taut in an embroidery hoop. Not only is it easier to handle, but the stitches will be more regular and distortion of the fabric will be kept to a minimum. If the area of embroidery is quite large, the hoop can be easily moved along the fabric after a portion of the stitching has been completed.

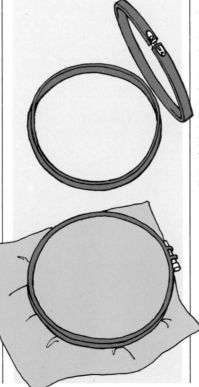

NEEDLES

Crewel and chenille needles are used for embroidery on fabric. They have larger eyes than ordinary sewing needles to accommodate a thicker thread. Crewel needles are of medium length and are used for fine and medium-weight embroidery. Chenille needles are longer and thicker, and have larger eyes than crewel needles, which makes them suitable for use with heavier threads and fabrics. Tapestry needles, which have blunt points, are used for working through the surface of some stitches.

All needles are graded from fine to thick, with the lower number denoting the thicker needle. The size of needle to use is really a matter of personal preference, but the eye should be large enough to let the thread pass through it without fraying. Always use a fine needle if you are embroidering on a light, delicate fabric.

THREADS

Embroidery threads are available in a wide range of weights and colors. The most common threads are made from cotton and wool, but pure silk, linen, synthetic, and metallic threads can also be bought. Some threads are tightly twisted and cannot be divided, whereas others are made up of several strands which can be separated to give a finer thread. The strands can be put together to give different weights and color combinations, or mixed with another thread. Some threads are not colorfast, so take this into consideration if the embroidered item is to be washed. If in doubt, work a few stitches on a scrap of fabric and wash it to check that the color is fast.

Two of the most useful threads are embroidery floss, which can be divided into separate strands (most stitches are worked best with three strands), and pearl cotton, which is twisted and must be used as a single thread.

TRANSFERRING A DESIGN TO FABRIC

① Use dressmaker's carbon paper in a suitable color for your fabric. It will work well on most fabrics and it is quick and easy to use.

② A transfer pencil will give a result similar to a commercial transfer. Take care to match the iron temperature to the composition of the fabric.

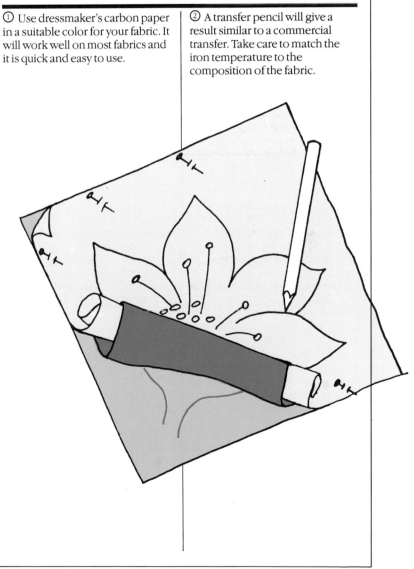

HERRINGBONE STITCH

Herringbone stitch is a line stitch that makes a pretty, crossed zigzag line. The stitches must be perfectly regular. It is worked from left to right and is very easy and quick to work. Guidelines may need to be marked on the fabric to keep the row straight. When the stitch is used as a filling, the rows can be placed so that the tips of the stitches on each row touch those on the row immediately preceding them. This will give a light trellis effect. For a heavier look, arrange the rows underneath each other so that the zigzags interlock. Herringbone stitch is also used as the foundation row for a number of more complicated stitches. Any type of thread can be used for this stitch, the choice depending on the size of stitch required and the weight of the ground fabric.

CHAIN STITCH

Chain stitch is one of the oldest embroidery stitches. Its use is widespread, and examples of the stitch can be found on many antique and contemporary textiles throughout the world.

Chain stitch usually forms a thin line. It can also be worked solidly to produce a dense filling, which lends itself well to shading. It is a simple stitch to work, but care should be taken to keep the stitches even and of the same size. Chain makes a good outline stitch and is very useful for defining curves and intricate shapes when worked quite small. Any thread is suitable, but the size of the stitch will depend on the weight of the embroidery thread used. Chain stitch can be used as a filling in either of two ways: it can be worked in close rows to fill the shape, or the rows can be worked from the center outward in a spiral, using one or more colors or textures. Chain stitch can have a row of backstitch worked down the center, in either a matching or a contrasting thread. Chain stitch can also be worked singly and it is then known as detached chain stitch or lazy daisy stitch.

CROSS STITCH

Cross stitch is probably the oldest and best known of all embroidery stitches. It has many variations and has been known world-wide for centuries. Cross stitch is still used on traditional embroideries in many areas, including the Greek Islands, Scandinavia, Central and Eastern Europe, and India.

It is extremely quick and easy to work and is used mainly on even-weave fabrics where the threads can be counted to keep the crosses even. The stitch can also be used on other plain-weave fabrics, but guidelines will need to be marked on the fabric unless a commercially produced transfer is being used. Among its many uses, cross stitch is excellent for outlines, solid fillings, formalized motifs, borders, and lettering. The top diagonal stitches must always fall in the same direction, unless a deliberate light-and-shade effect is required, in which case their direction can be varied to catch the light. Work a complete cross stitch before proceeding to the next stitch to form neat, slightly raised crosses.

STEM STITCH

Stem stitch is one of the most frequently used outline stitches. It is quite easy to work and follows curves and intricate linear details well. It can also be used for filling and shading areas.

The stitch is simply worked with a forward and backward motion along the line. The stitches should be evenly worked and equally sized. The working thread must always be kept at the right of the needle; if it is at the left, the effect is slightly different. A slightly wider stem stitch line can be made by inserting the needle into the fabric at a slight angle to the line instead of directly along it. Any type of embroidery thread can be used, provided that it is compatible with the size of the stitch and the weight of the ground fabric.

FEATHER STITCH

Feather stitch is a decorative line stitch. This stitch has been extensively used on traditional English smocks, both as a smocking stitch and as surface embroidery; it is also used as a decorative joining stitch on hand-sewn crazy patchwork.

It makes a pretty, feathery line, which is equally effective when worked in straight lines or following curves. Worked downward, it is a quick stitch, easy to perfect. The thread is brought through at the top of the line to be covered and a slanting loop stitch is made alternately to the left and to the right of the line. Any type of embroidery thread can be used with feather stitch but the desired effect and the weight of the ground fabric must be taken into account.

FANCY HERRINGBONE STITCH

Fancy herringbone stitch is a wide, ornamental stitch. It makes a rich border, particularly if a metallic thread is used for the interlacing, and it can look stunning if worked in spaced multiple rows, using a carefully chosen color scheme.

It is simple to work, in spite of its rather complex appearance. Each row is worked in three journeys. First, a foundation row of herringbone stitch is worked, using guidelines marked on the fabric. A row of upright cross stitches is then worked over the top and bottom crosses of the herringbone rows, taking care that the horizontal bar of the cross stitch is always worked over the vertical one. These two journeys can be worked in the same color thread, or two contrasting threads. On the third journey, the horizontal bars are interlaced without the ground fabric being picked up. Use a tapestry needle for the interlacing to avoid splitting the stitches on the two preceding rows.

FLY STITCH

Fly stitch is an isolated stitch often worked in rows. Each stitch is worked very easily: a V-shaped loop is made and then tied down with a vertical straight stitch. The tying stitch can vary in length to produce different effects. The fly stitches can be arranged side by side to make a horizontal row, or worked underneath each other to make a vertical row. The stitches can touch one another or be spaced apart at a regular interval. Isolated fly stitches can be used to make a pretty powdering, either spaced evenly or scattered at random over a shape. Each stitch can be decorated by the addition of a Chinese knot in a contrasting thread. Any type of thread can be used for this stitch, although the size of the stitch and the weight of the ground fabric must be taken into account.

TÊTE DE BOEUF FILLING STITCH

Tête de boeuf filling stitch is so named because of its resemblance to a bull's head, complete with the horns. A fly stitch makes the horns, and a single chain stitch anchors the fly stitch and makes the head. It is usually worked in formal rows to make an attractive light filling, but the stitch can also be worked in horizontal rows to form a border.

There appears to be some confusion about exactly which embroidery stitch is called tête de boeuf filling stitch. In some modern books tête de boeuf filling stitch appears under the name of detached wheat ear stitch, even though it looks exactly like a bull's head. However, the stitch described above can be found in many Victorian needlework books, including Caulfield and Saward's 1887 edition of *The Dictionary of Needlework: An Encyclopedia of Artistic, Plain and Fancy Needlework*, where a wood engraving of it and the reference "Tête de boeuf stitch" can be seen.

PEKINESE STITCH

Pekinese stitch is a composite line stitch. One of the principal stitches used on old Chinese embroideries, it was worked on a tiny scale, and was reputed to affect the eyesight of the worker, hence its alternative name, blind stitch. It was worked in silk and used to fill shapes solidly with carefully blended shades. Pekinese stitch makes an attractive braided line which follows any linear design well, and can be used as a filling stitch in the Chinese manner.

SATIN STITCH

Satin stitch is used for filling shapes and sometimes for borders. It is one of the oldest embroidery stitches and, like cross stitch, can be found worked on traditional embroideries in practically every country, but notably in China and Japan.

Satin stitch consists of straight stitches worked side by side. Although it appears to be an easy stitch to work, it requires some practice before it can be worked evenly. It should be worked on fabric stretched in an embroidery hoop to prevent the material from puckering, and the stitches should lie evenly and closely together to cover the ground fabric completely. When used for a border, it is worked between two lines with the stitches either slanting or at right angles to the lines to give a perfectly smooth surface. When worked to fill a shape, the stitches are taken right across the shape and can be worked vertically or diagonally, with changes of direction giving the effect of light and shade. This effect is enhanced by the use of a lustrous thread such as embroidery floss or silk, but any embroidery thread can be used, the choice depending on the effect required and the weight of the ground fabric.

CHINESE KNOT

The Chinese knot is an isolated stitch which closely resembles the better-known French knot, although the Chinese knot is flatter and more shapely. Chinese knots are characteristic of the rich silk embroideries of China, where they were worked very small and massed together to give texture to large areas. They were often worked in rows to create beautiful borders, with each row set close to the next one. Subtle color variations in the silk thread resulted in a delicate shading. The alternative name blind knot reputedly derives from the fact that Chinese embroiderers stitched this knot on such a minute scale over large areas of fabric that eventually their eyesight was affected.

The Chinese knot is easy to work, especially if the fabric is stretched in an embroidery hoop. A simple, loose loop is made around the needle and tightened after the needle has entered the fabric but before it is pulled right through. Hold the loop down on the fabric with the left thumb, while pulling the needle through the fabric. This stitch works well with any type of embroidery thread; choose the thread according to the effect desired. Embroidery floss or silk will give a flatter knot, whereas a rounded thread such as pearl cotton or tapestry yarn will make a raised knot.

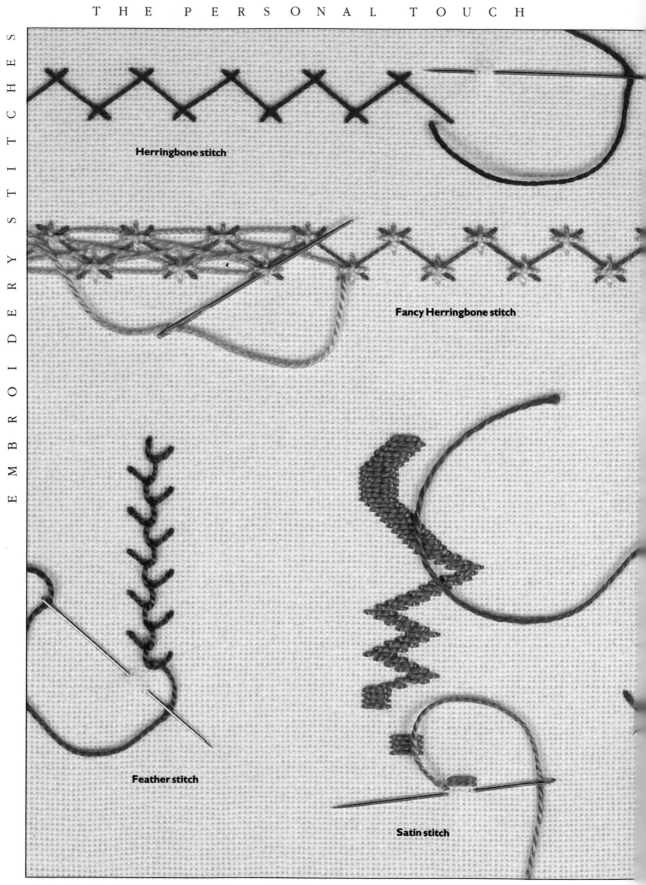

Herringbone stitch

Fancy Herringbone stitch

Feather stitch

Satin stitch

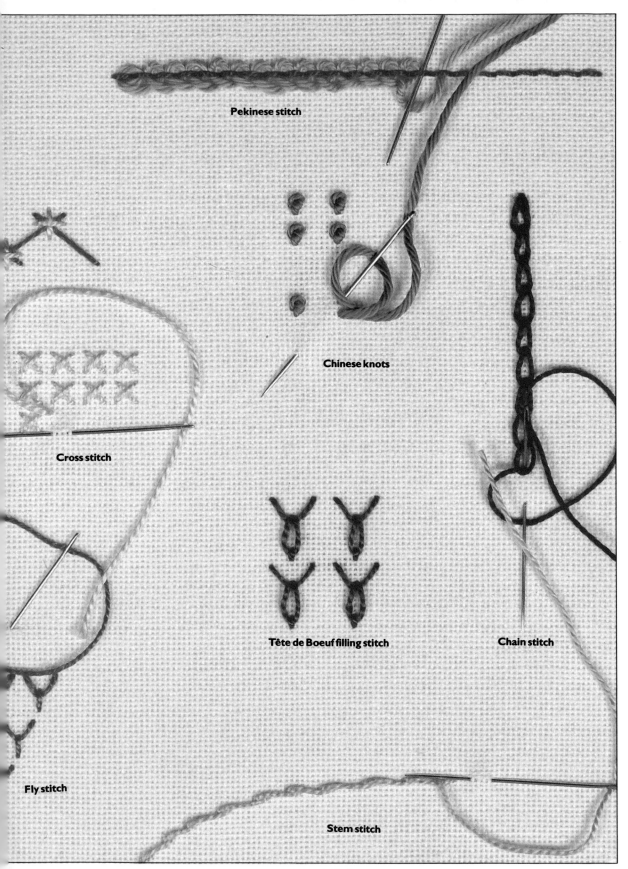

Pekinese stitch

Chinese knots

Cross stitch

Tête de Boeuf filling stitch

Chain stitch

Fly stitch

Stem stitch

M A C H I N E   Q U I L T I N G

There are two distinct types of quilting that can be worked successfully by machine. In the more familiar type, sometimes called padded quilting, two layers of fabric are separated by a layer of batting and then all three layers are stitched together in a design. This type of quilting adds warmth to a garment or bedspread as well as decoration. In the second type – corded or Italian quilting – only two layers of fabric are used, and the quilting is purely decorative. Two lines of parallel stitching make a narrow channel in the fabric and a fine cord is then inserted into the channel to make it stand out from the background fabric.

Choose simple, bold designs to quilt by machine and use closely woven, soft fabrics that are washable. Slippery and synthetic fabrics are tricky to handle and do not quilt well by machine. Polyester batting is ideal to use for padded quilting, since it will wash well without losing any depth. Never press a quilted item, or it will become flattened.

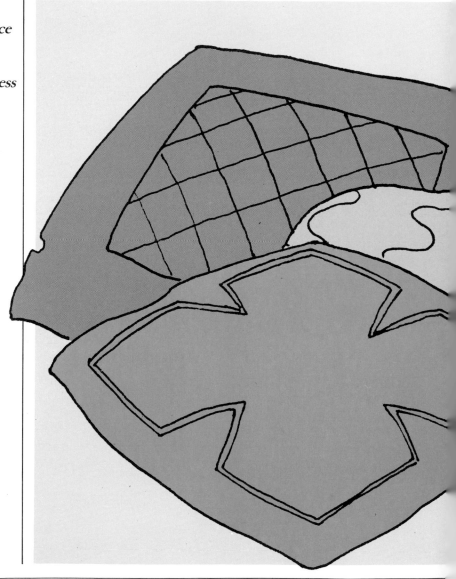

PADDED QUILTING

① Mark the design on the right side of the top layer of fabric with a marking pencil. Sandwich the batting between the two fabric layers and baste them together. Work the basting stitches horizontally and vertically at 4 inch (10cm) intervals across the layers, working from the center outward in each direction. Finish by working two diagonal lines from corner to corner.

② Loosen the pressure on the machine to allow the basted layers to pass easily beneath the foot. Stitch carefully along the design lines using straight stitch; pay particular attention to curves and corners. Remove the basting stitches when the quilting is completed.

CORDED QUILTING

① Mark the design onto the right side of the top layer of fabric with a marking pencil. Baste the two layers of fabric together as for padded quilting, with the wrong sides facing.
② Stitch along the design lines using a widely spaced twin needle and straight stitch. If your machine will not take a twin needle, work the two rows of stitching separately with a single needle.
③ Remove the basting stitches and thread pre-shrunk, fine filler cord through the channels using a tapestry needle.

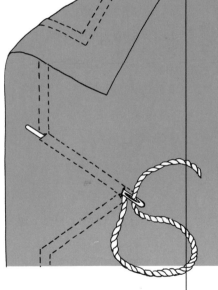

MACHINE APPLIQUE

Appliqué or applied work is a technique in which a motif cut from one piece of fabric is placed on a fabric background and stitched in place around the edges. The stitching can be decorative and hand worked, or done by machine.

Machine-stitched appliqué is hard wearing and probably best for items that will be laundered frequently. Match the weight and fiber content of the appliqué fabrics to that of the background, especially if the item is to be washed. Choose solid-color or patterned fabrics and cut the motifs on the straight grain where possible to avoid stretching. Apply the motifs before assembing the item, unless you are adding them to an existing item.

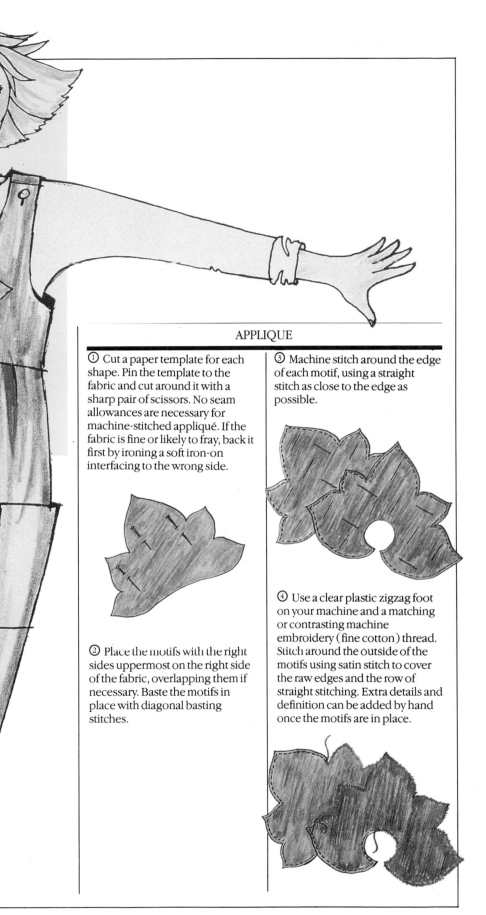

APPLIQUE

① Cut a paper template for each shape. Pin the template to the fabric and cut around it with a sharp pair of scissors. No seam allowances are necessary for machine-stitched appliqué. If the fabric is fine or likely to fray, back it first by ironing a soft iron-on interfacing to the wrong side.

② Place the motifs with the right sides uppermost on the right side of the fabric, overlapping them if necessary. Baste the motifs in place with diagonal basting stitches.

③ Machine stitch around the edge of each motif, using a straight stitch as close to the edge as possible.

④ Use a clear plastic zigzag foot on your machine and a matching or contrasting machine embroidery (fine cotton) thread. Stitch around the outside of the motifs using satin stitch to cover the raw edges and the row of straight stitching. Extra details and definition can be added by hand once the motifs are in place.

Patchwork is the art of stitching together small pieces of fabric to make a larger piece. One of the main attractions of patchwork is that you can use up scraps of fabric which are too small for anything else. There are two basic methods of construction patchwork. In the American block method, patches are joined with plain seams, right sides facing. Small units are joined in a logical sequence to make up the blocks, then the blocks are joined together. In the past this was done by hand and took many hours, but today the stitching can be done very quickly by machine. In English patchwork the patches are basted over paper templates and joined edge-to-edge by hand.

Patchwork is most often used for quilts, but it can also be made into garments and accessories like any other fabric, although it should be lined to conceal the raw edges.

SQUARES

Hit and miss
Castellated pattern
Framed squares

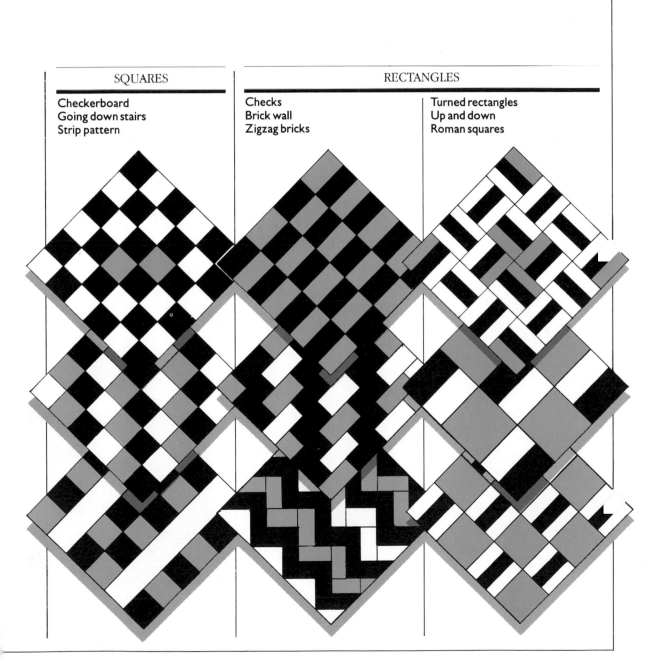

PATCHWORK DESIGNS

TRIANGLES

TRIANGLES AND SQUARES

High noon
Railroad crossing
Cotton reel
Birds in air

Jacob's ladder
Water wheel
Winged square
Ohio star

Shark's tooth square
Double T
Handy Andy
Boxed square

Rising star
Eight hand round
Lemoyne star
54-40

Greek cross block
Flying Dutchman
Tall pine tree
Weather vane

Red cross
Goose in the pond
Sherman's march
Rolling stone

MACHINE-STITCHED PATCHWORK

CUTTING THE PATCHES

① You will need to cut two accurate templates from stiff cardboard for every shape you are using. One template should be the size of the finished patch and the other should be ³/₈ inch (1cm) larger all around. Cut the two sizes of template from different colors of cardboard to avoid getting them mixed up when cutting the fabric.

② If you wish to center a fabric motif, cut a template with a cut-out window the size of the finished patch. Move it around on the fabric until it is in the right position and mark the fabric lightly around the window using a soft pencil.

③ Work out how many patches of each shape and color you need for the finished piece. Using the large templates and working on the wrong side of the fabric, draw around the shapes on the appropriate fabric with a soft pencil to mark the cutting line. Cut out the shapes and keep each color and shape of patch in a separate pile.

④ Center the smaller template on the wrong side of the fabric patch and draw around it with a pencil to mark the stitching lines. Keep the pencil sharp and follow the template shape carefully.

JOINING THE PATCHES

① Pin the patches together, following the sequence described below. Stitch along the pencil line and fasten off the threads at each end of the seam. Press each seam to one side before adding the next patch, preferably pressing the seam away from any light-colored patches.

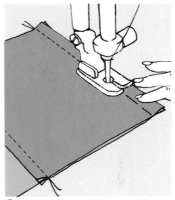

② Begin joining the patches together in pairs, and then add other patches until you have completed one section of the block. Join the sections together to make the finished block. Join the blocks into strips, and join the strips together to make the finished piece of patchwork.

MACHINE - STITCHED CRAZY PATCHWORK

Crazy patchwork is the original form of patchwork. It was probably invented as an economy measure to make something useful from worn-out garments. It is assembled rather like a jigsaw from randomly shaped patches which are pinned, basted, and then stitched to a firm backing fabric.

MACHINE-STITCHED CRAZY PATCHWORK

① Begin placing the patches at one corner of the backing fabric, starting with a right-angled patch. Gradually build up the design by placing the patches in turn on the backing so that they overlap the edges of the already positioned patches.

② The design can be worked in sections, by pinning and basting one area before moving on to the next, or all the patches can be laid out before they are pinned.

③ When all the patches are basted in place, work machine satin stitch over the raw edges. Use a clear plastic zigzag foot on the machine and take care to follow the outlines accurately.

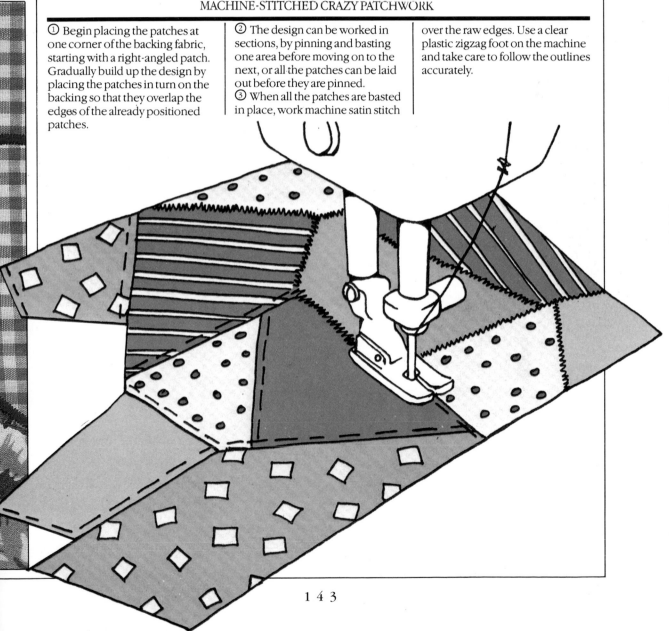

Many items of home furnishings are quite easy to make once you have mastered some of the basic sewing techniques described in Chapter 3. Bedlinen, comforters, tablecloths, draperies and cushions are less expensive to make than to buy, and you will have a much greater choice of fabrics and colors. This is especially important when you want to coordinate the color scheme for a particular room.

Tablecloths, napkins, and placemats are particularly easy for a beginner to make successfully. Table linen can coordinate or contrast with the table setting or the room décor, depending on the effect desired. Washable fabrics should always be used. Pure cotton, polyester/cotton and cotton/linen blends are all suitable for this purpose. When choosing the fabric, take into consideration whether you would like a crisp finish or a softly draped effect.

STRAIGHT-SIDED TABLECLOTHS

These are the most common and useful types of tablecloth; they can be either square or rectangular. They can be simply finished and functional or be decorated with embroidery, appliqué, lace, or braid. Patchwork tablecloths also look attractive.

① Measure the table top and decide how far you want the cloth to hang down over the sides. Add a 1¼ inch (3cm) hem allowance all around. If the fabric must be joined, avoid an unsightly seam down the center of the cloth. Cut out the center panel first, then cut another piece the same length and cut it in half lengthwise. Pin and stitch each half width to the sides of the center panel using a flat, self-finishing seam. Match any patterns on the fabric carefully.

② Press ⅝ inch (1.5cm) of the hem allowance to the wrong side along each side of the cloth. Fold over and press the second ⅝ inch (1.5cm) of the allowance. Open out the last hem fold and miter the corners.
③ Pin and stitch the hem. Alternatively, trim down the hem allowance to ¼ inch (5mm) and bind the raw edge of the cloth with a contrasting bias binding.

ROUND TABLECLOTHS

Round tables look particularly attractive when covered with a circular tablecloth. The cloth can overlap the table top by 12 inches (30cm) or so or it can reach the floor to give a more formal effect. Although it looks best if the cloth is cut from one width of fabric, it may need to be joined for a large table. Do this in the same way as for a straight-sided cloth.
① Measure the diameter of the table top first, and then the depth of the overhang. Double the overhang measurement and add it to the diameter. Add ⅝ inch (1.5cm) all around for the hem allowance.
② Fold the fabric into quarters and draw a quarter circle the required size on the fabric using a pencil and a piece of string, as shown. Alternatively, draw the quarter circle on a piece of sturdy brown paper, cut it out and use this as a pattern for cutting the fabric. Cut out the fabric.

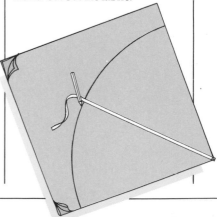

The usual size of a napkin is between 18 inches (45cm) and 20 inches (50cm) square, but they can be made in any shape or size, depending on your preference.
① Cut out the napkins. On each napkin, turn a double ¼ inch (5mm) hem on all the edges, mitering the corners.
② Pin, press, and stitch around the hem. Alternatively, bind the edge with bias binding as for a tablecloth.

PLACE MATS

Place mats are usually rectangular, measuring 8 inches (20cm) by 12 inches (30cm). They can also be round and measure between 8 inches (20cm) and 10 inches (25cm) across. Place mats should be thick enough to afford some protection to the surface of the table, so a quilted fabric is ideal. Buy ready-quilted fabric, or sandwich a thin layer of batting between the top and bottom layers of fabric before finishing the raw edges. You could also quilt your own fabric by hand or machine or use a piece of patchwork for the front.
① Cut out two pieces of fabric and one of thin batting of the required size, curving the corners slightly if the mat is rectangular.
② Place the fabric pieces together with the wrong sides facing, sandwiching the batting in between. Pin the layers together and baste around the edge.
③ Bind the raw edges with bias binding, following the instructions for binding a continuous edge.

③ Stitch around the outside of the cloth ⅝ inch (1.5cm) from the edge. This marks the finished edge of the cloth. On the wrong side of the cloth, press under the hem allowance along the stitched line. Pin, baste, and stitch the hem. Alternatively, trim down the hem allowance to ¼ inch (5mm) and bind the edge with a contrasting bias binding.

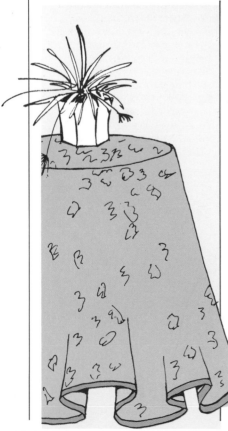

PILLOWCASES

You can make pillowcases for standard, queen, or king size pillows. Use a single piece of fabric for each pillowcase.

① Measure the length and width of the pillow. Double the length measurement and add 8 inches (21cm) for the flap and the hem allowances. Add 1¼ inches (3cm) for the seam allowance to the width. Cut out the fabric.

② Along one short edge, turn a double ¼ inch (5mm) hem to the wrong side. Pin and stitch in place. On the opposite short edge, turn 2 inches (5cm) to the wrong side and turn under the raw edge ⅜ inch (1cm). Pin and stitch in place, close to the inner fold.

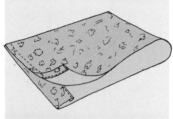

③ Lay the fabric out flat with the right side down. Fold in the edge with the narrow hem to make a 5½ inch (15cm) deep flap. Press and pin in place. Fold the fabric in half widthways with the wrong sides together, so that the other short edge with the wide hem is level with the flap fold. Pin and stitch the side edges, taking a ¼ inch (5mm) seam allowance.

④ Turn the pillowcase so that the right sides are facing as shown. Pin, baste, and stitch down the sides again, ⅜ inch (1cm) from the seamed edge. Turn the pillowcase right side out.

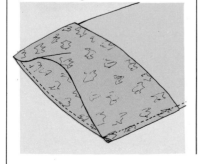

RUFFLED PILLOWCASES

This variation on the basic pillowcase features a pretty ruffle around the edges in matching or contrasting fabric.

① Measure the length and width of the pillow. Cut one back piece to this size, adding 2⅝ inches (6.5cm) to the length and 1¼ inches (3cm) to the width for the hem and seam allowances. Cut one front piece, adding a 1¼ inch (3cm) seam allowance all around. Cut a strip of fabric for the flap: the width should be 7 inches (17.5cm); the length should be two times the width of the pillow including seam allowance. Cut long strips of fabric for the ruffle to make a length twice that of the complete outer edge of the pillow. The width of this strip should be twice the width of the finished ruffle, usually between ¾ inch (2cm) and 3 inches (8cm), plus 1¼ inch (3cm) for seam allowances.

② Along one short edge of the back piece, turn under 2 inches (5cm) to the wrong side and then turn under ⅜ inch (1cm) along the raw edge. Pin, press, and stitch in place. Along one long edge of the flap, turn under a double ¼ inch (5mm) hem. Pin, press, and stitch in place. Pin, baste, and stitch the ruffle pieces, right sides facing, into a ring, using plain seams.

③ Fold the ruffle in half lengthwise with the wrong sides facing and pin. Divide the ruffle into four equal sections and mark. Gather each ruffle section in turn.

Divide the complete edge of the front piece into four equal sections and mark. Position the ruffle on the right side of the front with the ruffle inward to the center. Pull up the gathering stitches of each section in turn to match the sections on the pillowcase front. Match the marks on the front to those on the ruffle and then pin, baste, and stitch the ruffle in place.

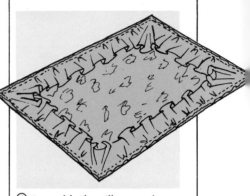

④ Assemble the pillowcase by placing the back on top of the ruffled front with the right sides facing. Align the hemmed edge of the back with the seamline on the front. Place the flap right side down over the back, as shown, matching the long raw edge with the raw edge of the front. Pin, baste, and stitch in place, following the previous line of stitching; take care not to catch the hemmed edge of the back in the stitching. Trim and finish the raw edges, remove the basting stitches, and turn right side out.

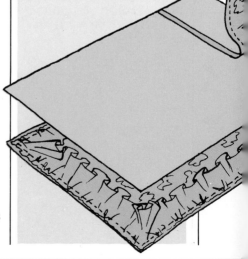

S H E E T S

There are many attractive items you can make for the bedroom. Making a bedspread or quilt in fabric to match your curtains or draperies is one way to coordinate your decorating scheme. Or, if you have a down comforter, you could make a cover for it. You can even make your own comforter, at a significant saving. Sheets and matching pillowcases are other items you may wish to make. The furnishing fabric and dress fabric departments of a good store will offer many possibilities for giving your bedroom a well-coordinated look.

FLAT SHEETS

Flat sheets are the simplest type of sheet to make.
① Measure the mattress across the top in both directions, adding twice the depth of the mattress and a 10 inch (25cm) tucking-in allowance to both these measurements. Add 8 inches (20cm) to the length and 1½ inches (4cm) to the width for the hem allowances. Cut out fabric.

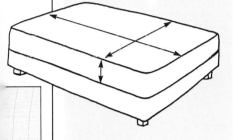

② Turn under a double ⅜ inch (1cm) hem on each side edge. Pin, press, and stitch in place. At the base end, turn a double 1 inch (2.5cm) hem to the wrong side, and pin, press, and stitch in place.
③ Turn a double 3 inch (8cm) hem to the wrong side along the top edge, and pin and press in place. Using a cording foot, zigzag stitch over a length of fine cord approximately ⅜ inch (1cm) from the inner fold of the hem. Fasten each end of the cord securely. Alternatively, work two rows of straight stitching ⅛ inch (3mm) apart to form a channel. Thread the cord through the channel with a fine tapestry needle.

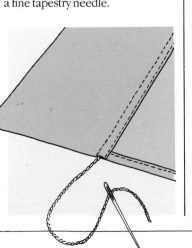

FITTED SHEETS

Fitted sheets have elasticized corners and they are ideal for the lower sheet on a bed. They need to be measured accurately to give a good fit.
① Measure the mattress top both ways, and to both of these measurements add twice the mattress depth plus twice the tucking-in allowance of 7 inches (18cm). Cut out the fabric.
② Make each corner seam first. Measure the mattress depth plus 7 inches (18cm) along each side from the corner and mark. Measure in at right angles from the two marks as shown, and mark again. Fold the marked corner with the wrong sides facing; pin and baste. Cut off the corner of the fabric as shown, leaving a ⅝ inch (1.5cm) seam allowance. Make a French seam along this edge to form the corner seam.

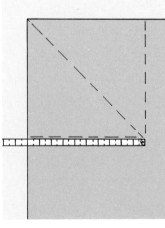

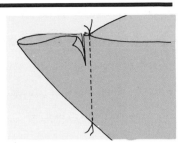

③ Turn under a double ⅝ inch (1.5cm) casing around the edge of the sheet and pin in place. Measure along the casing for 13½ inches (34cm) on each side of each corner seam and mark. Baste and stitch around the casing, leaving a ⅝ inch (1.5cm) opening at each mark.

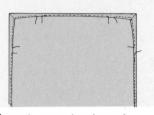

④ Cut four 9 inches (23cm) lengths of narrow elastic. Pin the end of one length of elastic at one opening inside the casing. Thread the opposite end of the elastic around the corner inside the casing and pin at the other opening.
⑤ Pin and stitch across the casing and ends of elastic just before the openings; use two rows of stitching to hold the elastic firmly. Stitch across the openings to close neatly. Repeat at each corner.

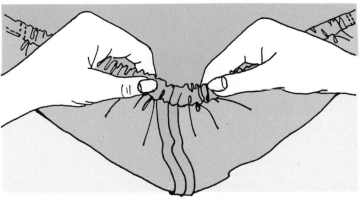

C O M F O R T E R S

Down comforters are warm, light, and comfortable to sleep under, and they are becoming increasingly popular. However, they are rather expensive. You can save money by making your own, using down or feather and down filling, or a synthetic filling.

The comforter is a fabric bag divided into walled channels, which keep the filling in place. If you are using a feather filling, use downproof cambric, with the shiny side inside, for the bag. If you are using a synthetic filling, any lightweight, closely woven cotton will do. White cotton tape, 2 inches (5cm) wide, or strips of fabric is used for the walls of the channels.

Traditional comforters are filled with sterilized duck or goose down, either by itself or mixed with feathers for economy. Synthetic fillings have the advantage of being washable, so they are ideal to use for children's quilts, as well as for people who are allergic to feathers.

The fabric bag is made in exactly the same way for both natural and synthetic fillings, but the method of filling is slightly different. A full-size comforter measures 80 inches (200cm) by 80 inches (200cm), and a single comforter is 55 inches (140cm) by 80 inches (200cm). If the fabric has to be joined, use a flat fell seam.

MAKING THE COMFORTER BAG

① Cut out two pieces of fabric the size of the finished comforter, adding a ¾ inch (2cm) seam allowance all around. On the wrong side of each piece of fabric, mark the stitching line ¾ inch (2cm) from the edges.

② Mark the position within the finished area of the channels on each piece of fabric. Rule lines with tailor's chalk to divide the width into equal sections. On a twin-size comforter make five 11 inch (28cm) sections, and on a full-size comforter make eight 10 inch (25cm) sections. Cut an 81½ inch (204cm) length of cotton tape for each marked line on one piece of fabric.

③ Working on one piece of fabric, place the first length of tape over the first marked line, overlapping it by ¼ inch (5mm). Pin and stitch the tape to the fabric ¼ inch (5mm) from the edge of the tape. Repeat this with the remaining lengths of tape. Place the two

pieces of fabric together with the right sides facing, matching the side edges. Pin, baste, and stitch

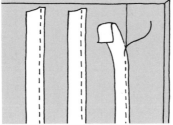

along one margin line parallel to the tapes to make the first side seam.

④ Working away from the stitched side seam, join the free edge of the first piece of tape to the second piece of fabric, again overlapping

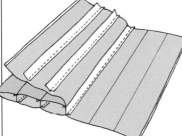

the marked line by ¼ inch (5mm). Repeat this on each free edge of tape, as shown.

⑤ On the open side of the comforter, fold both pieces of fabric together into a double ⅜ inch (1cm) hem. Pin, baste, and stitch along the hem twice, the first time close to the fold and the second about ¼ inch (5mm) away from the fold. Hem the base edge of the comforter in the same

way. Along the stitched side seam, work two rows of topstitching to match the stitching on the hemmed side edge.

FILLING THE COMFORTER

Allow the following amount of filling per channel (approximately):
Pure down – 5oz (150g)
Down and feather (60% down/40% feather – 6oz (175g)
Feather and down (60% feather/40% down – 7oz (200g)
Synthetic filling – 7oz (200g)

① Pin the top edge of the comforter to a clothesline, making sure that the channels are open. If you are using a feather filling, put a handful of filling into each channel in turn, closing the channel with a clothespin after each handful. Repeat this until all the filling has been used.

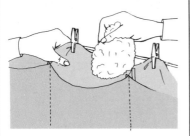

② For a synthetic filling, first divide it into equal portions for each channel. Fill each channel in turn, pinning them closed after they are filled.

③ In either case, fold the open edges together to make a double ⅜ inch (1cm) hem. Baste and stitch twice to match the other edges.

COMFORTER COVERS

It is a good idea to use a cover on a comforter, to keep it clean and help prolong its life. If you are making your own cover, the easiest method is to use two sheets, trimming them to the required size; otherwise, you will have to join widths of fabric. The cover should be slightly larger than the comforter. Add 5 to 7 inches (13 to 18cm) to the width of the comforter and about 2 inches (5cm) to the length. For fastening the cover use a length of snap tape or ribbon ties.

① Cut out two pieces of fabric the required size, adding a seam allowance of $3\frac{5}{8}$ inches (9cm) to the length and $1\frac{1}{4}$ inches (3cm) to the width. Fold a double 1 inch (2.5cm) hem along the base of both pieces. Pin, baste, and stitch.

② Place the two pieces of fabric together with right sides facing, matching the hemmed edges. Pin, baste, and stitch together along the inner edge of hem for 12 inches (30cm) in from the side edges, to make a central opening.

③ Place a length of snap tape along one half of the hem opening. Pin, baste, and stitch in place. Repeat this for the other side of the opening, making sure that the snaps align.

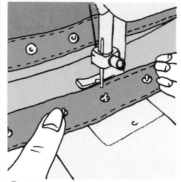

④ Fold the cover with the right sides facing. Pin, baste, and stitch twice vertically across the hem at each side of the opening to enclose the raw edges of the tape. Fold the cover with the wrong sides facing and make a French seam around the other three sides. Turn the cover right side out.

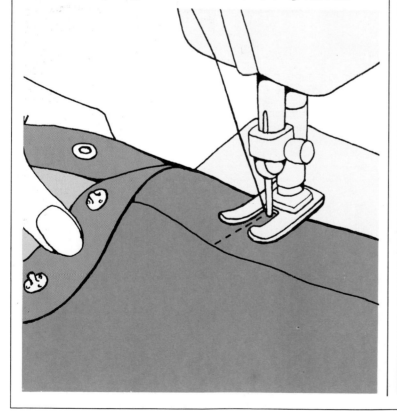

B E D S P R E A D S

There are three main types of bed coverings: throw bedspreads, fitted bedspreads with a gathered flounce, and tailored bedspreads. A throw bedspread is simply a flat piece of fabric that is draped over the bed, and this is the easiest type to make. The other two are more formal.

They all have a full fabric width on the top, to which side panels will need to be attached to give the correct width for a full-size bed. Cut out two fabric widths to the required length, allowing extra on the length for matching the pattern if necessary. Cut the second piece in half lengthwise and join the half widths to the sides of the center width with a plain seam. Finish the raw edges of the seams.

Any type of fabric can be used for a bedspread, but a firm fabric will give a better result than a fine, delicate one and it will not need to be lined, except for a gathered fitted bedspread. You should always make up the bed fully before measuring it to estimate the fabric requirements.

THROW BEDSPREAD

This simple bedspread should be large enough to cover the bed and reach to the floor. The corners can be rounded to give it a neater appearance and the seam along the bed top can be corded in a matching or contrasting fabric.
① Measure the made-up bed widthwise to the floor on both sides. Measure lengthwise from the headboard to the floor. Add a 2 inch (5cm) hem allowance all around.
② Cut out the fabric, and join it if necessary. Turn 2 inches (5cm) to the wrong side and turn under the raw edge for ⅜ inch (1cm). Press the hem and miter the corners. Pin, baste, and machine stitch hem. Remove the basting and press the hem.

GATHERED FITTED BEDSPREAD

This type of bedspread is very pretty, but it needs much more fabric than a throw spread and it is more complicated to make.

① Measure the top of the bed both ways and add 7¾ inches (20cm) to the length for the tuck-in and 1¼ inches (3cm) to the width for the seam allowances. To calculate the length of the flounce, add twice the bed-top length to the bed-top width and then double this measurement to allow for the gathering. For the depth of the flounce, measure from the bed top to within ⅜ inch (1cm) of the floor and add 1¼ inches (3cm) for the seam allowances. The length of fabric for the flounce will need to be joined, so allow extra fabric for seams and pattern matching.

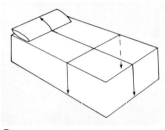

② Cut out the fabric and then cut out a second set of pieces from lining fabric. For the lining, use a soft cotton fabric that harmonizes with the main fabric.

③ Round off the fabric and lining for the bed top at the base corners. To do this, draw around a plate and then cut along the marked line. Join the main flounce pieces with flat seams and repeat this for the lining flounce pieces. Press the seams well.

④ Place the fabric and lining flounce pieces together with the

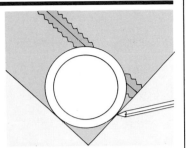

right sides facing. Pin, baste, and stitch them together along the side and base edges. Turn the flounce right side out and press. Pin and baste the top raw edges together.

⑤ Divide the length of the flounce into six equal sections and mark them with tailor's tacks. Divide the side and base edges of the bedspread top into six equal sections and mark in the same way. Stitch two rows of gathering between the marks on the flounce, and pull up each section to fit the marked sections on the top.

⑥ Place the flounce on the bedspread top with the right sides facing and the sides of the flounce ⅝ inch (1.5cm) from the straight edge of the bed top. Cording can be added before you pin, baste, and stitch the flounce in place.

⑦ Pin, baste, and stitch the top straight edges of the lining and fabric bedspread top together, with the right sides facing. Press the seam and turn the lining down over the wrong side of the top. Turn under the side and base edges of the lining and pin to the wrong side of the flounce, covering the previous line of stitching and the raw edges. Baste the lining in place and slipstitch it to the lining of the flounce.

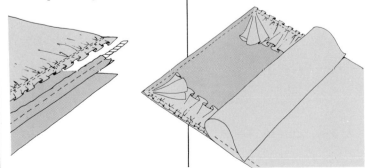

TAILORED BEDSPREAD

This type of fitted bedspread is quite plain in its construction and looks best with the pillows placed on top. The seam around the top can be corded to give a crisper finish.

① Cut out one piece of fabric for the bedspread top to the measurement of the bed top, adding 1⅞ inches (4.5cm) to the length and 1¼ inches (3cm) to the width for seam allowances. For a full-size bed, you will need to join two lengths of fabric to get the correct width. For the depth of the sides, measure the distance from the bed top to within ⅜ inch (1cm) of the floor and add a 2⅝ inch (6.5cm) hem and seam allowance. Measure the side edges of the bedspread top and the base edge, and add 1¼ inches (3cm) to each measurement. Cut out two pieces of fabric for the sides and one for the base.

② Join the side and base pieces to make a long strip, using plain seams and taking a ⅝ inch (1.5cm) allowance. Press the seams. Turn up a double 1 inch (2.5cm) hem along the lower long edge and pin and stitch it in place. Press the hem.

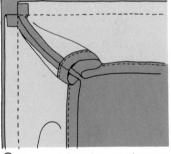

③ Placing right sides together, pin the strip to the top. Match the seams to the corners and, before stitching the corners, undo ⅝ inch (1.5cm) of the seams on the strip to allow the fabric to lie flat. Stitch, taking ⅝ inch (1.5cm) seams, and pivot the fabric when stitching the corners. Press the seams toward the top and finish the raw edges.

④ Turn up a double ⅝ inch (1.5cm) hem along the top edge of the bedspread, and pin and stitch it in place.

PILLOW FORMS AND COVERS

Pillow forms can be bought ready-made, but the shapes and sizes available are rather limited. They are quick to make, and you can make virtually any shape, including rectangles, circles, triangles, stars, and shell shapes. Fill them with either a feather and down mixture or polyester fiberfill which is less expensive. Foam chips are also available, but they tend to be rather hard and lumpy. An old feather pillow or down comforter makes a good source of pillow filling. If you are using a feather filling, make the cover of the pad from featherproof cambric, placing the shiny side inside. For other fillings, a strong unbleached muslin is adequate.

PILLOW FORMS

As a guide, for an 18 inch (45cm) square pillow you will need a little over 2.2 pounds (1kg) of feather and down mixture or 1 pound (450g) of polyester fiberfill.

① Cut out two pieces of fabric of the required shape and size, adding 1¼ inches (3cm) all around for the seam allowance. Place the pieces together with the right sides facing and pin, baste, and stitch around the edge, leaving an opening of at least 7¾ inches (20cm) in the center of one side.

② Stitch around a second time to strengthen the seam. Trim the seam allowance to ⅝ inch (1.5cm) and turn the cover right side out. Stuff the cover firmly. Take care to stuff the corners of triangular and star-shaped cushions firmly. Turn in the raw edges of the opening in line with the seam and slipstitch to close. Use small stitches and a strong thread to prevent the pillow from splitting.

RECTANGULAR PILLOW COVERS

Basic rectangular pillow covers are easy to make, and they can quickly provide a splash of color in a room. For decoration, add cording or a ruffle in a contrasting color or type of fabric.

① Measure the pillow form each way. Cut out two pieces of fabric to the required size and add a ⅝ inch (1.5cm) seam allowance all around. Place the two pieces of fabric together with the right sides facing, and pin, baste, and stitch together all round, leaving an opening in the center of one side.

② Trim the seam allowance to ⅜ inch (1cm) and cut across the corners close to the stitching. Finish the raw edges. Turn the cover right side out.

③ Insert the pillow form. Turn in the raw edges of the opening in line with the seam and slipstitch to close. If you want to remove the pillow cover for laundering there are various alternative ways of closing the opening.

OPENINGS

① Make an opening across the center of the cover back by making a plain seam and inserting a zipper using the centered method . This

works especially well on a corded cover. You will need to add an extra 1¼ inches (3cm) to the seam allowance on the back when cutting out the fabric to allow for the center seam. Omit the side opening when making the cover.
② Follow the instructions given for making a plain European pillowcase, but make the flap much deeper.

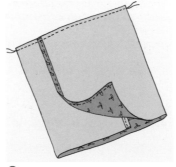

③ Use snap tape or a length of nylon tape to fasten a side opening. Make the opening on the pillow cover in the same way as for a comforter cover.

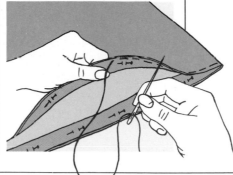

SHAPED PILLOW COVERS

Shaped pillow covers are made in the same way as rectangular ones. The opening can be along one edge or on the center of the back, depending on your preference.
① Cut out two pieces of fabric of the same size and shape of the pillow form plus ⅝ inch (1.5cm) seam allowances all around. Make as for a rectangular cover.

Making your own curtains and draperies is much more economical than buying custom-made, or even ready-made, ones. The range of fabrics available is extensive – from lightweight sheers suitable for frilly tiebacks to the most elegant heavy brocades for a formal living room. The basic sewing techniques are not difficult; all you need is a certain amount of patience in handling large quantities of material.

Draperies can be lined or unlined. If they are sheer, they are not lined. If they are opaque, however, it is a good idea to line them. A lining helps them to hang more smoothly, guards against fading, and provides another layer against drafts. Cotton sateen is the fabric normally used for lining.

When buying fabric for curtains or draperies that will be washed, make sure that it is shrinkproof. If you are in doubt, buy a little extra and immerse the fabric in hand-hot water for a few minutes before cutting out. Always check the fiber content of the fabric and make sure that you know what kind of care it requires.

If you are buying a patterned fabric, remember that you will need to match the pattern at the seams and where the edges of the curtains or draperies meet at the center.

Matching large patterns will usually entail buying a considerable amount of extra fabric. Ask the salesperson to advise you on how much extra you will need.

Draperies are usually floor-length, although some informal draw draperies hang just below the sill. Glass curtains are also usually floor.length, but other styles of curtain may just reach the sill or hang slightly below it. Café curtains are hung from a point halfway up the window.

DRAPERY HARDWARE

When you are planning your window treatment, visit a good-sized department store and see the various kinds and the hooks and other hardware designed to be used with them. The simple flat curtain rod, which is made of metal, is adjustable for different widths of window and is used with the kind of curtain made with a casing. Double rods are available for crisscross curtains. Café curtains are hung from a decorative round metal pole.

Decorative poles are used these days for both draw and panel draperies. They provide an attractive finishing touch above the heading and are less complicated and often less expensive than adding a valance or cornice. They are available in various styles and sizes to suit your décor. Some of these are simply poles, designed to be used with large rings and suitable for panel draperies or café curtains that will usually remain stationary. Those intended for draw draperies are really disguised traverse rods – the rings are attached to the cords concealed in the pole.

Conventional flat traverse rods are adjustable for different widths of window and are invisible once the draperies are hung.

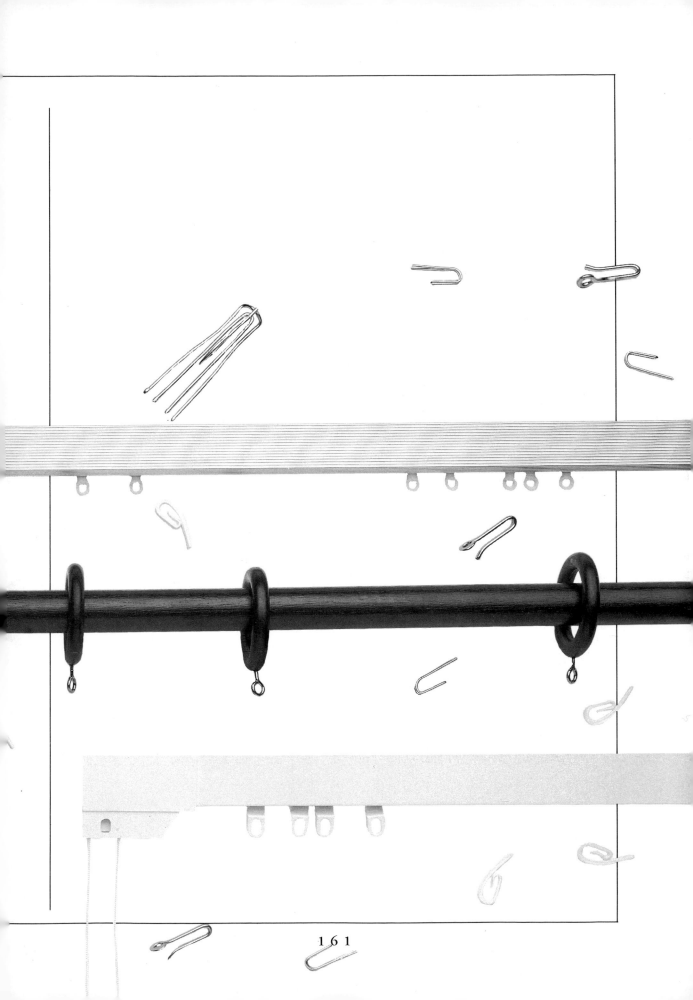

D R A P E R Y   H E A D I N G S

Draperies can be pleated by hand, for an extra-elegant look; but special heading tape will do a lot of the work for you and gives excellent results. The kind of tape usually used produces triple pinch pleats and is made with narrow pockets into which four-pronged pleater hooks are inserted. In some stores you may also find English tape, which is made in several other styles, producing pencil pleats, cartridge pleats, and gathers. These tapes include cords, which are pulled up to pleat or gather the draperies.

GATHERED TAPE

Gathered tape is the simplest heading and is suitable for informal rooms. It is fairly narrow and gathers the fabric randomly. This type of heading needs about one and a half times the rod length of fabric.

STANDARD TAPE

Standard tape is the simplest and most economical heading to use. It is fairly narrow and gathers the fabric randomly for an informal look. This type of heading needs about one and a half times the track length of fabric. Standard heading is ideal for use on unlined curtains, as it comes in different colours and can be used on all types of fabric. There is a special lightweight standard tape for use with nets and sheer fabric.

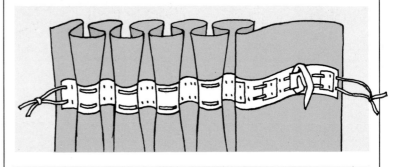

PENCIL PLEAT TAPE

This type of tape gathers the fabric into regular tight pleats. It can be used on all weights of fabric and requires between two and a quarter and two and a half times the rod length of fabric. It is available in various widths and has two or three lines of pockets so that the hooks can be placed in different positions to suit the type of rod.

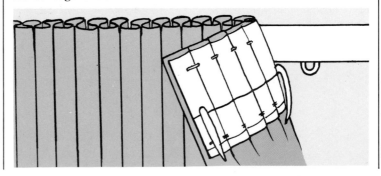

CARTRIDGE PLEAT TAPE

This type of tape is particularly suitable for use with heavy fabrics such as velveteen and brocade. It gathers the fabric into evenly spaced rounded pleats and requires two and a half times the rod length of fabric.

TRIPLE PLEAT TAPE

By far the most popular heading, this gives an elegant, formal look suitable for traditional and modern styles. The tape requires approximately two and a half times the rod length of fabric.

LINING TAPE

Lining tape is designed specially to attach a detachable lining to a drapery. The lining is sandwiched between the two layers of the tape and the lining tape is then hooked onto the drapery tape. It requires about one and a half times the rod length of lining.

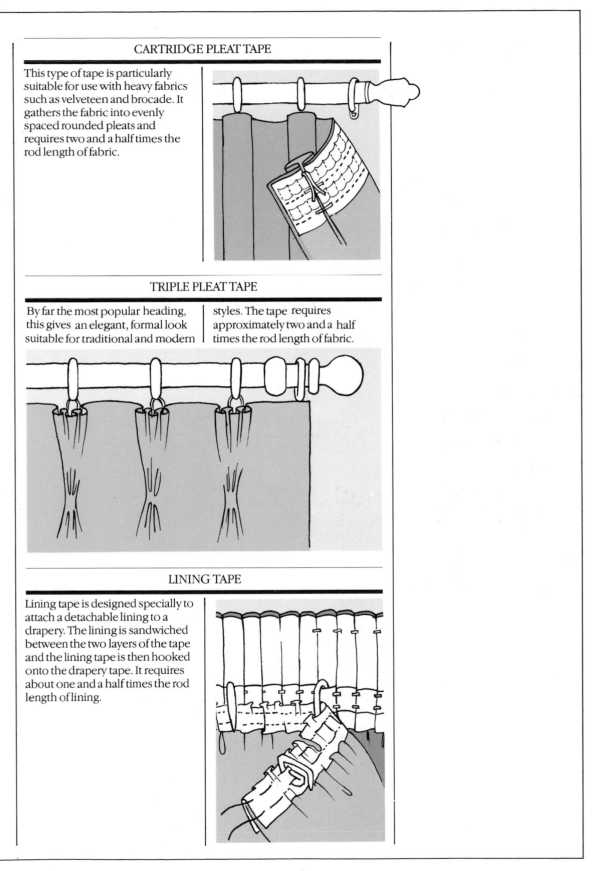

MEASURING WINDOWS AND CUTTING THE FABRIC

MEASURING WINDOWS

① Fix the rod or pole above the window before you begin to measure.

② Decide which heading tape you will be using, since this will determine how many rod lengths of fabric you need. Divide the total width needed by the fabric width (usually 54 inches, 137cm) to find out how many widths will cover the rod.

③ To find the length of each fabric drop, measure from the rod to where you want the drapery to end. If the draperies are to be floor-length, subtract $5/8$ inch (1.5cm) to allow the drapery to clear the floor. Add the allowance for the top (depending on the heading tape you are using) and at least $5\frac{1}{2}$ inches (15cm) for the hem. If the fabric is patterned you will also need to add the length of one pattern repeat for each drop after the first one. This will allow you to match the patterns correctly.

④ Multiply the length of the drop by the number of fabric widths to find the total amount of fabric required.

⑤ You will also need to buy enough heading tape for the width of the drapery plus extra for adjusting the pleat positions and for turning under.

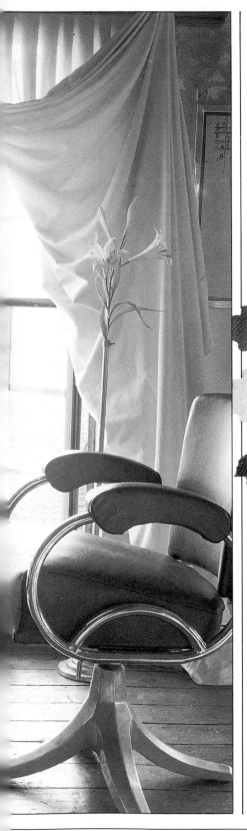

SOLID-COLOR FABRICS

① Straighten one cut edge of the fabric along the grain. Measure the first length from the straight cut edge and mark across the fabric using a yardstick and tailor's chalk. Cut across the marked line and repeat for each length.
② Cut any half widths of fabric by folding the fabric in half lengthwise with the selvages together. Carefully cut along the fold.

PATTERNED FABRICS

① Always place complete motifs along the base edge of the curtain, since any half motifs at the top will be partially hidden by the pleat folds. Mark the base of the pattern repeat and measure the hem allowance below this mark. Cut along this line.
② Place the cut length against the uncut fabric and match up the pattern across both widths. Mark and cut off the second length to match the first one. Repeat this for each fabric length. Cut any half lengths as for solid-color fabric. Mark the top of each length to make sure that they are all the same way up before you begin making up.

UNLINED DRAPERIES

Unlined draperies are the easiest type of draperies to make. They can be used at most windows, although there will be a danger of fading if they are made of cotton and exposed to strong sunlight.

Detachable linings can be added to make the draperies warmer during the winter. A detachable lining is also preferable to a normal lining if the draperies are to be washed rather than dry cleaned, since they will be less bulky to handle.

① Cut out the fabric lengths. Allow 5½ inches (15cm) for the base hem and heading and 1½ inches (4cm) for each of the side hems. Trim the selvage from each side of the fabric lengths. This will prevent the finished drapery from wrinkling along the seams and side hems.

② Pin the fabric widths together if one width is not sufficient, taking care to match pattern, if any. Position half widths of fabric on the outside edges of the draperies. Baste and stitch the seams using a plain seam and matching thread. Finish the raw edges and press the seams open. Turn in ¾ inch (2cm) along the side edges and 2 inches (5cm) along the hem edge and press.

③ Miter the corners on a double folded uneven hem as follows: measure twice the hem width above the folded hem edge and mark with a pin on the folded side edge. Measure twice the side hem width from the folded side edge and mark with a pin on the folded hem edge. Fold in the corner point over the single hems from pin to pin and press well.

④ Turn in a further ¾ inch (2cm) along the side edges and 2 inches (5cm) along the hem edge and press well. Slipstitch the folded edges together at the corner. Pin, baste, and slipstitch the side and hem edges, using a matching thread and small stitches.

⑤ Lay the drapery flat with the right side up. Measure up from the hem edge and mark the finished length of the drapery at intervals across the drapery width using a yardstick and tailor's chalk. Turn the surplus fabric to the wrong side along the marked line and press.

⑥ Place the heading tape against the top folded edge according to the manufacturer's instructions, trimming any excess from the fabric as necessary. Leave an extra ¾ inch (2cm) to 1¼ inches (3cm) of heading tape at each side for finishing. Pin the tape in place. At the inside edge of the drapery, pull out the heading tape cords on the wrong side of the tape and knot each one securely. Trim this raw

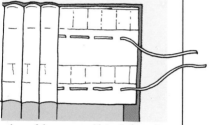

edge of the tape to ⅜ inch (1cm), including the knotted cords, and fold it under. At the outside edge of the drapery, pull out the cords from the front of the tape, trim the surplus tape to ⅜ inch (1cm) and turn it under, leaving the cords free.

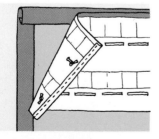

⑦ Baste and stitch the heading tape in place following the stitching lines if they are marked on the tape. Take care not to catch the loose cords at the outside edge of the drapery in the stitching. Stitch along the top and bottom edges of the heading tape in the same direction.

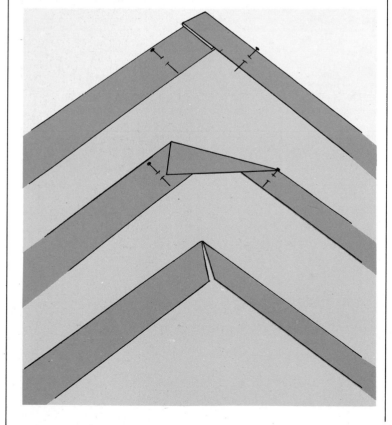

DETACHABLE LININGS

Detachable linings are made with a pocketed tape that shares the same hooks as the draperies and is meant to be used with draperies made with corded heading tape. The appropriate drapery hardware is sold for this purpose.

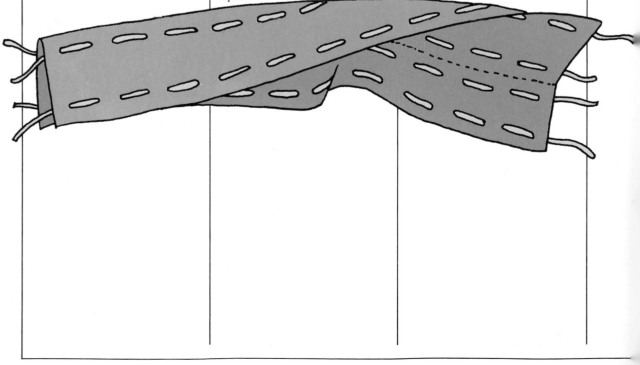

① Cut out and make the linings in the same way as for unlined draperies, apart from the top edge.
② Measure the length of the lining so that it will be 1 inch (2.5cm) shorter than the drapery. Mark this length at intervals across the width using a yardstick and tailor's chalk. Cut across the marked line.
③ Slip the cut edge of the lining in between the two parts of the tape. Pin, baste, and stitch along the tape.

Lined draperies look very professional and they will hang better than unlined draperies. Circular weights can be added to heavy fabrics at the corners of the drapery and the base of each seam.

① Cut out the fabric as for unlined draperies, allowing 7¾ inches (20cm) for the bottom hem and heading, and 2½ inches (6.5cm) for each side hem. Cut out the lining in the same way, but cut it 5½ inches (15cm) shorter and 5 inches (13cm) narrower than the drapery fabric.

② If necessary, join the fabric widths in the same way as for unlined draperies and then repeat this for the lining. On the drapery fabric, turn in 2½ inches (6.5cm) on the side edges and 5½ inches (15cm) along the bottom hem and press. Miter each bottom corner and secure it with slipstitching. Pin, baste, and herringbone stitch along the side and bottom hems using matching thread.

③ Lay the drapery fabric flat with the wrong side up and mark the vertical center line down the length of the fabric using a yardstick and tailor's chalk. Mark lines 12 inches (30cm) apart on

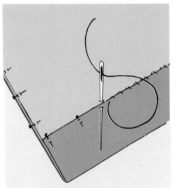

each side of the center line. With the wrong sides facing, center the lining over the drapery fabric with the raw edges matching the top, side and hem edges of the drapery fabric. Pin the lining and drapery

fabric together along the central marked line.

④ Fold back the lining against the pins and lock stitch it to the fabric down the center line, using matching thread. Begin stitching 4 inches (10cm) from the top raw edge and continue to within ¾ inch (2cm) of the fabric hem. Repeat this along each marked line, working outward from the center in each direction.

⑤ Pin and baste the lining and drapery fabric together along the top raw edge. Turn in ¾ inch (2cm) down the side edges of the lining and 2 inches (5cm) along the base edge. Press and pin the turned edges.

⑥ Slipstitch the lining to the drapery fabric along the side and base edges, using matching thread and small stitches. Finish the drapery in the same way as for an unlined drapery, turning down the top edges of the lining and drapery fabric together.

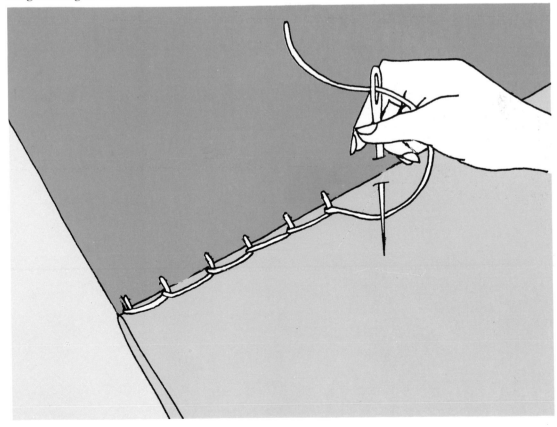

CAFÉ CURTAINS

Café curtains are short curtains that are usually fixed halfway down the window. They can be made from a sheer fabric in the same way as unlined draperies, using pleater tape. Another method is to make one flat, ungathered curtain with a scalloped top and attach it to a pole with curtain rings.
① Cut out the fabric to the required size and then make the curtain as for an unlined drapery panel, allowing an extra ⅝ inch (1.5cm) at the top and leaving the top edge unfinished. Divide up the width of the top edge to ascertain the number of finished scallops it will hold. 3 inch (8cm) scallops with ¾ inch (2cm) bands between each one are usual, with wider end bands.
② Make a paper pattern of the scalloped edge, as shown, and use it to mark the position of the scallops with tailor's chalk on the wrong side of the curtain top, ⅝ inch (1.5cm) from the raw edge. Divide the remaining fabric into two equal parts for the end bands.

③ Cut out a facing 1¼ inches (3cm) wider than the curtain and 2⅝ inches (6.5cm) deeper than the scallops. Turn under ⅝ inch (1.5cm) along the bottom and side edges of the facing and press. Place the facing against the curtain with the right sides together and the curtain uppermost. Pin, baste, and stitch along the marked line.
④ Cut out the scallop shapes ¼ inch (5mm) outside the stitched line. Trim corners and clip seam allowance at curves. Press and turn the facing to the wrong side of the curtain, gently pushing out the corners of the bands with the point of a knitting needle so that they are really square. Slipstitch the sides and bottom edge of the facing to the curtain.

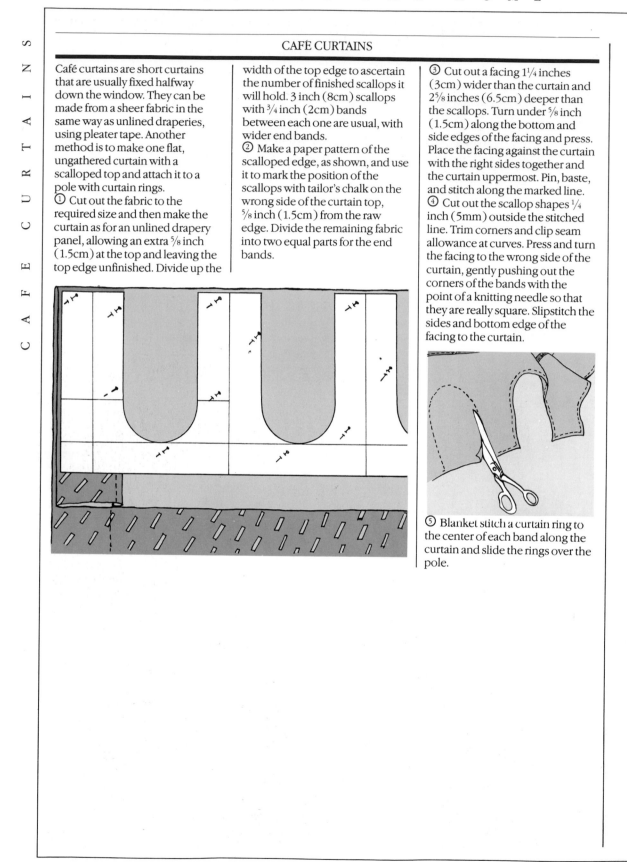

⑤ Blanket stitch a curtain ring to the center of each band along the curtain and slide the rings over the pole.

CREDITS

The photographs on these pages have been reproduced by courtesy of the following:

140	Spike Powell, Elizabeth Whiting & Associates (*Quilt by Gillian Newbury*)
144, 158	Michael Nicholson, EWA
147, 164	Christine Hanscomb
149	Michael Dunne, EWA
150	Gary Chowitz, EWA
152	Tim Street-Porter, EWA
155	Collier Campbell
156	Michael Crockett, EWA
167	EH/EWA
171	Home Improvements, EWA

All other photographs are the property of Quarto Publishing Limited